SHIPBOARD PERSONNEL MANAGEMENT

SHIPBOARD PERSONNEL MANAGEMENT

G. SHEKHAR

ANMOL PUBLICATIONS PVT. LTD.
NEW DELHI - 110 002 (INDIA)

ANMOL PUBLICATIONS PVT. LTD.

H.O.: 4374/4B, Ansari Road, Darya Ganj,
New Delhi-110 002 (India)
Ph.: 23278000, 23261597

B.O.: No. 1015, Ist Main Road, BSK IIIrd Stage
IIIrd Phase, IIIrd Block
Bangalore - 560 085 (India)
Visit us at: www.anmolpublications.com

Shipboard Personnel Management

ISBN 978-81-261-3203-4

PRINTED IN INDIA

Printed at Mehra Offset Press, Delhi.

Contents

Preface

'Shipboard Personnel Management' is a comprehensive study of marine laws, workforce organization and staff management. This is a first hand book which deals with recruitment procedures and training courses in this rich field.

The marine engineering is growing day by day. This needs a highly technically men power to support all departments of the industry. It is in this context students need to undergo proper education and training. Keeping in this point in mind, this book shipboard personnel management is written to cater all the needs of the aspirant students. We have made a indepth study of different marine courses and laws relating to Marine Engineering. This book is equally beneficial to people who are interested in a carrier in Marine Engineering

Personnel Management is a vast area of study which covers human behaviour office approach, Organizational skill and recruitment, but in course of Shipboard Personnel Management, Special physical skill and training is very essential. At times laws relating to Marine recruitment are very hard and Government interference is a recurring factor.

Shipboard Personnel Management-the present book discusses all areas relating to recruitment, law and management.

Hope our labour will bear fruit.

Author

Preface

Chapter 1

Introduction

It has oft been asked by those ashore how a ship operates, who is in-charge and ignorance shines forth when an engineer is asked "and when will you become Captain"! It is therefore time to lay-to-rest some of these myths and to give explanation as to what foundation a ships management structure is based upon.

Every business whether it is a high-flying banking firm or the local plumbers outfit a management structure in place. In a smaller ad-hoc company down the road the management structure may consist of one man sitting in an office, who barks out order like a sniffer dog struck lucky, to a down trodden son who has no choice in the matter or a large wall street firm that has hundreds of workers, many VP's, directors and a chairman who nobody ever sees.

Whatever company looked at there is a structure in place, whether it is the ideal structure and whether it works or is practical in real life is not important except to say that like all businesses, cruise ships, gas tankers, ferries, rowing boats and offshore supply vessels all have a management structure in place.

A vessels management structure is extremely defined! It is built on decades of culture and formulation and has adapted and changed with time to produce a system that is at first glance ideal, it covers all aspects of shipboard operations and lifestyles and is tightly regulated through strict control from ashore. A seafarer cannot rise up the ranks of structure to a higher position unless he has sat and passed the requisite number of exams, he cannot become a self-imposed boss through financial wangling, bribery or luck or through the showing of family wealth to impose authority.

The only way that any seafarer can climb the management structures ladder is to have the right qualification and the only way to get the right qualification is to study at college, pass a written exam or two and be interrogated by an experienced surveyor who should know what he is talking about. Even this might not be the last step to increased authority; the company primarily must approve the promotion subject to availability, suitability and requirement. It is only recently that officers are able to sail in a higher position upon receipt of their new qualification due to the shortage of seafarers worldwide. Ten, even twenty years ago, many officers of junior rank would hold the highest available ticket yet be unable to sail in that position. They might hold that ticket for five or more years before a position came available and they were promoted.

Many people assume from having watched weird films(set on a ship that is mysteriously plummeting to the sea-bed with a pack of rabid dogs onboard or sea snakes overtaking a vessel as steams along) that authority is defined by the number of stripes one wears on their shoulders. Certainly, this noted fact is distinct on many vessels, the higher up on the ladder one is the more stripes they have to weigh them down; after the Titanic disaster Engineers were eventually acknowledged as being integral to the operation of a vessel and were given officer status (represented by purple stripes to the outside of the gold). But uniforms are not necessary, they are merely a status symbol, a method used to implement authority and structure but with or without the uniform the structure remains in place.

Uniforms might be necessary on ships were large crews operate, where faces are often unrecognizable amongst the crowd and so the wearing of a badge identifies one immediately in the position that they hold. On smaller vessels though were perhaps only ten or so officers and crew live in confined quarters the emphasis these days is on integration not segregation, to produce a more family orientated atmosphere so that life onboard is not wrought with ill-will.

The wearing of a uniform is not an integral part of the management structure. The structure is defined through the rank that one holds and this is clear to all concerned, there is no wavering of this structure, there is no option to change and like it or lump it if a person comes onboard with a certain rank then that is the position that he or she will assume. In a similar situation ashore, if a finance-orientated guy with all the appropriate qualifications is offered a job as Chief Financial Officer then he will expect and be expected to fulfill that role when he sits in the chair. He would certainly not like to find himself relegated to the basement as mail boy on his first day and nor would the company like to find out ten weeks down the line that he couldn't add 2 + 2 never mind run accounts!

The management structure is divided into paths! The Captain has the ultimate authority on a vessel! The Captain is after all responsible for safe operations, the safety and well-being of his crew and will answer any questions asked regarding improper actions, unsafe work practices, oil pollution and accidents that may occur whether or not he was involved or even out of his bunk at the time. For example; if an Able Seaman gets drunk and beats up the cook during an argument then the Captain will be called to account. If the Chief Engineer overfills his bunker tanks and floods the Humber River with prime gas oil then the Captain will be looking for a lawyer from inside of the local nick! The position comes at a heavy price!

Under the Captain is the Chief Officer who will one day hope to become Captain or who will remain as a Chief Officer for the rest of his career if he does not feel that the responsibility that tags along is worth the price.

The Captain, the Chief Officer and in descending order the Second Officer and Third Officer (sometimes referred to as Deck Officers or Navigation Officers or by Engineers as Deck Tarts) are all trained as navigators! They are responsible for the safe navigation of the vessel, they are responsible for the stability and integrity of the vessel, for cargo operations (unless it gets too difficult for them and the engineers have to take over) and for ensuring that the correct paperwork is completed and filed for ships business relating to the above and as that defined by the office.

There is though another path or two to follow at sea, not everything is about navigation and form filling. The path of engineering and before anybody asks again, "no, a Chief Engineer cannot become a Captain"! Or to re-phrase that, he can become a Captain if he goes back to school and studies for three years, goes to sea in a junior rank for one year, then studies some more and then hopes that he gets promoted to a not so junior rank and then sails some in this rank and then studies some more at college and hopes that he passes and gets promoted to cut a long story short; should an engineer wish to become a navigating officer he would have to study and sail as a deck officer for a number of years and it might be ten or more years before he would sit in the Captains chair. The same works the other way around, a deck officer cannot wake up one morning and decide that he would prefer to go downstairs rather than up, a career path has been chosen and to change would involve a mass of financial input (which no company would entertain) and time.

The Chief Engineer is responsible for the maintenance of the vessel, the operation of its machinery and the fabric of the boat. He, like the Captain has worked long and hard to reach the position that he has attained and with this position comes the fact that he is second in command of the vessel and again that responsibility weighs heavily on his shoulders. He in turn is backed up by a second, third and fourth engineer who will all hopefully one day climb that ladder to fill the Chiefs shoes.

On typical trading vessels these are the two command lines of the management structure. There are other specialties, an electrician maybe included onboard and his responsibility will lie with anything electric, to maintain it in a desired safe and operable condition. He will remain an electrician throughout his career, neither gaining nor dropping in rank and will be on a par to the third engineer. Varying vessels might have other ranks to consider, fridge engineers, radio officers or cargo specialists, all are of middle rank and all fit into the structure underneath the top two, the Captain and the Chief Engineer.

Finally, yet equally important are the crewmembers, an integral part of the management structure with each sailor arriving onboard with appropriate training, experience and skills that make the back-bone of any boat, so to speak! Each department has the requisite number of able seaman, the deck has sufficient to handle cargo work, lookout and watch duties, the engine room has an oiler or two to look after the cleanliness of the machinery spaces and to provide needed support to the engineers. The cook may have a galley boy or girl to help with the washing of the dishes and to clean the officer's cabins, hopefully he or she will one day rise up to become a cook, should they so desire. It must be remembered that crew members are integral to a vessels operation, some may rise up the ladder in years to come (though study and financial input) but generally speaking they are the work force and will remain crew members throughout their career.

This is the management structure! It is not open to discussion, it is set down on paper and like it or lump it this is the way it works. There are many occasions when the boundaries are crossed, when personalities clash or experience talks but the one underlying factor that inhibits excessive out-of-rank behavior is that with each rank comes a pre-defined responsibility so by either inflating oneself to a position of higher than given or deflating oneself down the ladder it does not change the rank structure or the inherent responsibilities tagged to it. If a mate starts barking orders to the engineers or changing course of the vessel without authority from the master he better have a good reason for doing so! If he did these actions without due cause, (maybe for the safety of the vessel) then he will find himself on the next plane home. If the Second Engineer decided to stop the engine for a bit of piece and quiet without first discussing this with the Chief Engineer then the world will come crashing around his ears! In addition, let us not forget, if an Able Seaman decides that he likes to drink coffee out of the Chief Officers personal cup, then he might find himself looking out for yellow submarines from the f/castle in a force nine gale!

In a similar situation ashore, a company for example that has directors, managers and a work force, all go home each night. The actions of the chef who decided that he should send an email on behalf of the supply manager to order 7000 pairs of high heels shoes, might find himself looking for another job or suffering the wrath of another, but he has not endangered lives and he has not crossed boundaries that could influence the health and safety of other souls. And should the financial director decide to walk into the interior design section of the company one day and make an order that the toilets should be painted black on all floors, the workers will probably find that there toilets are all painted black within the next few days. The financial director will happily sign the chit for the paint, the workers will not say boo and the company won't blink an eye, he is the financial director after all. Nothing will even be said at the next directors meeting. The other directors will probably snicker and grumble behind his back but nothing will result and the toilets will remain black until some other director gets it into his head that they should be blue.

The rank structure or management structure is extremely defined at sea purely and simply because of the lack of links to ashore. The need for well-defined authority and the need to preserve that authority are required and without which the system would fail. If the system fails, the safety of the ship and its crew are at stake. One of the ways to preserve the rank structure is through strict regulation over the requirement to have a certain qualification to fill any rank, the higher you go the more you need.

Stepping ashore again, the Chief Planner in a factory may find that the assistant planner has ambitions. The Chief Planner may come to work one very average morning to find that his assistant planner had gone and implemented a plan that the Chief Planner had himself planned. The end result of the outright usurp of authority might be that the Chief Planner very shortly find himself reading the Jobs page in the local rag simply because the planning director liked the plan that the assistant planner had said he had planned. Not to get confused with all the plans, this obviously fictitious example has only been laid out to show one things: that qualifications ashore in a management structure are often of no importance. The chief planner could have had a degree in zoology, the assistant planner a bus-ticket it would matter not!

Ships have a very defined and on the table management structure, it is one that has worked for many decades and one that will be around for a lot longer to come. It has become fact that many companies ashore are looking toward engineers to run floating installations, were the rules-of-the-sea do not come into force and there are mutterings that engineers have a more diverse background, able to command a larger number of tasks and are therefore preferred in a shipping company management positions ashore - some of these murmurs might just be true. It may also be mentioned that Oil and Water don't mix but despite this inconsequential banter and despite the continuing interference of the outside world, the management structure onboard is set in concrete for some time to come, it holds itself well through rough weather and bad and it rides smoothly into the troughs and sits proudly on the peaks - the shipboard management structure has a solid foundation!

Shipboard Life

By the early sixteenth century, Europeans had heard about the rich fishing grounds off the Grand Banks of Newfoundland. Due to the numerous meatless days imposed by the Catholic Church, fish was in great demand. The coastal waters off Europe had been severely overfished, creating food shortages, so by the mid-sixteenth century, French, English, Spanish, Portuguese, and Basque ships began crossing the Atlantic to fish and hunt whales. Hundreds of ships and thousands of men were employed each year catching and processing cod off the Grand Banks.

Each year, Breton and Norman fishermen came to fish on the banks of Newfoundland. These cod fishermen cast their lines from the deck of their ship. Without ever setting foot ashore, they cleaned and salted enough fish to fill the hold. This was called the "green cod fishery." The green, or fresh, method of processing cod is illustrated in a life-size diorama in one of the exhibits. Four men are standing in barrels to avoid being tossed overboard and to protect themselves from dampness, which caused a disease called "black leg," a severe form of arthritis. They are cleaning the cod, throwing the entrails overboard, and packing the fish in large barrels containing salt to preserve it.

The Basques from northern Spain and southwestern France were the most active whalers at the time. They established a dozen whaling stations on the southern coast of Labrador, along the Strait of Belle Isle.

Each spring, hundreds of ships with a crew of approximately 1,000 men would make the four-week crossing to Terra Nova for the annual whale hunt. These expeditions usually ended by late November to avoid the winter ice, but sometimes ships would depart too late or freeze-up would come early, forcing them to spend the winter in Labrador. Insufficient protection against the cold, unhealthy living conditions and an inadequate diet took a toll on the number of sailors that survived the winter. Such was the fate of Joanes de Echaniz. On Christmas Eve 1584, he dictated his final will and testament from his ship, which was trapped in the ice at Terra Nova. The scene is recreated inside the ship's hold in the exhibition.

Monitoring Shipboard Management Ashore

Taking into account the recent advances in improving satellite bandwidth connectivity for ocean going vessels, it is believed that the near future vessels will be connected "almost online" to the head office ashore in almost the same manner that stores, factories and warehouses of any land based corporation are connected online today. Yes seafarers, big brother could soon be watching your every move, as the world's fleet look set to have the same level of IT connectivity as the rest of the land-base industries. Worldwide coverage is also expanding at a rate, which makes the whole communication area more practical for real time information sharing resulting in the streamlining of operations.

Paul Ostergaard, Founder and Chief Executive Officer, ShipServ, believes that in three years the majority of shipping Companies with more than ten vessels will be managing their ship supplies electronically, including interacting electronically with their suppliers. By the end of this decade, most shipping companies will be transacting electronically with all their trade partners. "The future requires successful companies operate in a flexible, alert and efficient manner to strengthen their market positions and meet the growing global competition", says Lone Jenson, marketing Co-ordinator, ShipServ.

"The vast implications of this forthcoming change and profound improvements in efficiency and speed of operations" says Dr. Panagiotis Nomikos, Businees Development Director, Danaos Management Consultants. Danaos is the only Maritime Software provider who has tested vigorously its onboard systems via broadband vessel connections in several vessels over the past two years.

Those vessels are operating the software in always-on connections, like any other land-based network node. As yet, not all ship managers have succumbed to purchasing shipboard management systems but as the costs come down they will no doubt find them much more attractive as they come under increasing pressure from demands and requirements as set by IMS, ISPS, TMSA and the classification bodies to name but a few. "The Maritime Industry is growing rapidly in terms of use of information technology and it is only a matter of time until all ships have state of the art systems on board providing operational efficiency and safety at sea," believes Per Steiner Upsaker, Manageing Director, Bass who see the future are bright for shipboard management systems.

BASS applications systems have been used since 1997. "We started of our system being built on Visual Basicand our database on Oracle and SQL Server," says Upsaker. The company have made a significant step forward since 2003 in re-development of their product suite into the Microsoft.Net platform, a robust, reliable and future-proof technologiacal platform for software development. "For Document management, safety/quality management and accident/ incident reporting-.Net development is now well on its way to provide customers with "state-of-art" applications," adds Upsaker.

One such happy customer is Dampskibsselskabet Torm. "SAFIR 4.0 enables us to establish, define and track actions related to enhancements of safety and quality on board our ships," says Per Winther Christensen, Safety and Quality Manager of the Danish Company. SAFIR 4.0 is a strong reporting and analyses tool that complies with the requirements of section 9 of the ISM Code and supports the implementation and maintenance of the ISPS Code, ISO 9000 and ISO 14000 systems.

BASS provide an intelligent and robust ship-shore replication mechanism, which synchronises the shipboard databases with the office database. The communication costs are low- as only the data- changes are transmitted, even for procedural changes in documents ashore/ onboard. Additionally, the in-built auto-scheduling and auto-recovery functions of the ship-shore replication-enable seafarers and office staff to stay in synch and work "real-time" without spending time on ship-shore monitoring and trouble-shooting.

So have faster, cheaper communications helped the development of shipboard management systems?

Its a long-term benefit and a short-term obstacle believes Capt. Michalis Hatzimanolis, Marine Expert, Marketing and Pre-Sales, Ulysses Systems. "Cheap communications initially results in unstructured communication and communication overload." With added structure, cheaper communications result in more precise coordination, performance support and transparency. Shipboard management systems have benefited from cheaper communications but since communication is so much cheaper in land based industries; the adoption of shipboard software is still impended by the discontinuous nature of communications.

Nonetheless with all this talk of being "permanently connected" between ship and shore the question, which all seafarers must be speculating about, is just how controlling will Big Brother turn out to be when he is keeping a close eye on operations? As communications have improved over the years, many masters have already voiced their annoyance at, what they perceive to be an increasing interference from the office, which they state, undermines their professionalism to do the job that they trained for. It remains to be seen whether this increased state of monitoring will worsen the situation.

Chapter 2

Personnel Management in Shipboard

Personnel management as a term describes those activities that are necessary in the recruiting of a workforce, providing its members with payroll and benefits, and administrating their work-life needs. In many locales, these activities can require a considerable amount of regulatory knowledge and effort, and many enterprises can benefit from the recruitment and development of personnel with these specific skills.

Personnel management is both an academic theory and a business practice that addresses the theoretical and practical techniques of managing a workforce. The theoretical discipline is based primarily on the assumption that employees are individuals with varying goals and needs, and as such should not be thought of as basic business resources, such as trucks and filing cabinets. The field takes a positive view of workers, assuming that virtually all wish to contribute to the enterprise productively, and that the main obstacles to their endeavors are lack of knowledge, insufficient training, and failures of process.

PM is seen by practitioners in the field as a more innovative view of workplace management than the traditional approach. Its techniques force the managers of an enterprise to express their goals with specificity so that they can be understood and undertaken by the workforce, and to provide the resources needed for them to successfully accomplish their assignments. As such, PM techniques, when properly practiced, are expressive of the goals and operating practices of the enterprise overall.

The basic premise of the academic theory of PM is that humans are not machines. Therefore we need to have an interdisciplinary examination of people in the workplace. Therefore fields such as psychology, industrial and organizational psychology, sociology, and critical theories: postmodernism, post-structuralism play a major role. Many colleges and universities offer bachelor and master degrees in personnel management.

Academic Theory

The basic premise of the academic theory of PM is that humans are not machines. Therefore we need to have an interdisciplinary examination of people in the workplace. Therefore fields such as psychology, industrial and organizational psychology, sociology, and critical theories: postmodernism, post-structuralism play a major role. Many colleges and universities offer bachelor and master degrees in human resources.

Critical Theory

Critics of PM have noted that PM suffers the problem of the connotation of its own name; treating humans as a resource. However, some are trying to change the name of the field to Human Capital.

Rhetoric has had an important consideration within the understanding of critical theory, of the rhetorics and realities PM (Legge 2005). Postmodernism and post-structuralism theories play an important part here because we can consider the importance of understanding and contemplating the reality of language and understanding.

Management Gurus have tried to have the effect of attempting to move academic theory into a sellable product, which management gurus and consultants can sell to business leaders.

Some critics have noted that in practice, while the philosophy PM has changed the workplace, the department or manager who used to have "Personnel Manager" on their door, has now changed that sign to "Human Resource Manager" and that is the only change.

Empowerment has been noted as a PM practice which by critics has been noted more as a pseudo-empowerment, based on attitudinal shaping. Other such PM practices have been noted as hidden within rhetoric, and many examples particularly within Call Centers are much more Orwellian, and hide the reality, through attitudinal shaping.

Personnel Management is part of a business or company which recruits, develops and utilizes an organization's personnel in the way which would benefit the firm's objectives. Creating alignment between an organization's HRM strategy and the core objectives of a business is seen to be essential.

Personnel Management of Independent Contractors

The Personnel management of the contingent workforce can be challenging due to the unique legal and operational landscape. There is much research indicating the benefits and advantages to working as and hiring independent consultants. Companies benefit because they can hire a highly skilled and experienced expert to work on a short-term project and do not have to hire the consultant full-time. The benefits of this are that the company incurs a relatively low cost, because they pay a rate to the consultant for exactly and only the amount of time they are needed. The alternative to this would be hiring the consultant permanently and having to pay for the time the professional is not working on a major project. Many industries now have a rising need for the flexibility and speed of deployment of skilled contractors, and permanent talent can never fill this demand. Also the company gets an experienced professional to work on the project, most likely resulting in a finished product of high quality.

The independent consultant benefits because he or she may choose when and where to work, on which projects to work (probably those in which he or she is most interested) and can also choose his or her salary by negotiating a competitive billing rate. There are, however, several challenges in managing independent consultants in regards to human resources. The hired consultant often does not work in the same physical office space of the hiring client, and therefore could be rather detached of the company. Also the contractor works for the company for a short period of time. These aspects of the independent consultant's profession could present HR problems in terms of lack of motivation, lack of cohesion with the hiring company's goals and culture, as well as miscommunication between the consultant and his or her manager or director.

From a security standpoint, the independent consultant is somewhat of a "foreigner" in the company and may pose concerns about his or her trustworthiness. Also, if the company does not correctly classify the contractor (for example if they were hired as an independent, but are really considered an employee), it is at risk for IRS Reclassification. Although these are legitimate concerns and real challenges, there are several solutions and ways to succeed in the management of independent contractors. For temporary administrative workers, Staffing companies can fulfill the HR need. In the case of more specialized consultants (highly skilled and highly compensated experts), a better solution is to use a Portable Employer of Record or an Umbrella company.

PRINCIPLES OF CONTROLLING SUBORDINATES AND MAINTAINING GOOD RELATIONSHIP

One of the concerns of personnel management is the assignment of personnel on the basis of capacity and interest to perform specific functions, tasks, and duties. It involves recognizing that every individual uses a basic knowledge, skill, or ability in performing a task and these capacities should be fully used. You should be able to exercise your leadership responsibilities in dealing with these human relations. Leadership can be defined as the ability to direct or influence the behavior of others toward specific goals. In carrying out this mission, your responsibilities do not stop with the assignment of duties and the delegation of authority. You must also control the functions.

One of the most difficult tasks facing a supervisor is making a fair and efficient distribution of individual jobs among assigned personnel. If this could be done by a simple mathematical formula (jobs ÷ available personnel = distribution), it would present no problem.

However, it is not that simple. Your personnel will have varying degrees of knowledge and experience. Also, the jobs differ in complexity, required time to perform, and frequency of performance. While the ultimate responsibility for the assignment of personnel rests with the supply officer, this officer will rely heavily on your recommendations. What Are the Jobs? The first step in planning personnel assignments is to prepare a list of all jobs that are to be given to suitable persons of your trust.

The following are examples of frequently seen displays of undesirable motives:

- Trying to save time and effort
- Trying to maintain personal comfort
- Trying to express resentment

An undesirable motive is clearly a complex problem. A person does not react simply to the basic needs of comfort, security, belonging, and self-fulfillment. Attitudes, feelings, and emotions stemming from a multitude of sources also affect a person's motives.

Lack of Training and Experience

Mishaps caused by a lack of training and experience occur most often when people tackle a task with which they are neither familiar nor qualified. Experienced personnel can clearly recognize hazardous conditions that inexperienced persons may not notice. Since the inexperienced persons' limitations then exceed their capabilities, a mishap may occur. The imbalance between a person's skills and required levels of training shows through improperly followed procedures, shortcuts, errors in judgment, and improper maintenance and operations. Supervisory personnel sometimes contribute to mishaps by making assignments without adequate knowledge of the capabilities and limitations of their people and equipment.

When you are training inexperienced people for new jobs, their training needs are obvious. They need your help to gain the knowledge and skills they must have to do a job. Even when you provide people with the basic skills to do a job, they may not thoroughly understand it. They may be unable to retain what you taught them. You must counterbalance this lack of understanding with close supervision. As people become more experienced and less closely supervised, training deficiencies become more apparent. Finding people placed in tasks beyond their current skill development is not uncommon. When asked if they can handle the assignment, many respond positively. They do not want to appear incompetent. Knowledge alone is not always enough to prevent a mishap. Most tasks in the Navy require a certain skill level. These skills can vary from those required to paint a bulkhead to those required to operate a nuclear reactor. To properly accomplish any job, people must safely develop skills through practice.

Interpersonal Relationships

Since interpersonal relationships with our peers, supervisors, spouses, and parents can affect our mental attitudes and moods, they can contribute to mishaps. A worker's distraction because of worry about a pending divorce can lead to a mishap. A worker's disregard of an order because of a personality conflict with management or a supervisor can result in a mishap too. To avoid being labeled a "wimp," a person may give in to peer pressure and purposely take risks, such as working without eye protection. That can also result in a mishap. When you investigate the causes of a mishap, carefully consider the personal lives of the people involved. Are they having problems at home? Are they under pressure because of financial troubles? Could peer interaction possibly have contributed to the cause of the mishap?

Maintenance and Support Factors

Maintenance and support factors include improper maintenance, improper priority assignments on work requests, or lack of proper quality assurance. Shipyards, intermediate maintenance activities, contractors, or a ship's force may be involved with maintenance and support. Mishaps can result from the way the manufacturer made, assembled, or installed the equipment. They can result from premature equipment failure caused by a manufacturer's improper processing and fabrication, improper assembly, or use of improper materials. Mishaps can also result from part failures caused by a manufacturer's deviation from design specifications, such as incorrect size, weight, strength, and similar engineering characteristics. Material damage and personal injury mishaps can result from improperly maintained equipment. A motor incorrectly rewound at a shipyard could short out and cause a fire. Improper QA or the lack of approved QA procedures can result in a mishap. These types of mishaps overlap with human error causes.

List of the general qualities and skills necessary for a successful management candidate

1. Interest in developing personal management skills and helping others develop appropriate
2. Ability to work in harmony with people - must understand people, must be able to deal with both individuals and groups, and must be able to supervise them without creating undue tension.
3. Understanding basic concepts - a grasp of the principles of management planning, organizing, delegating, directing and controlling human resources, budget, equipment, and instruction.
4. Integrity - an honest, straightforward attitude is essential to a good working relationship with employees. Employees quickly recognize deceit and react to broken promises.
5. Emotional maturity - a manager must have the flexibility to adjust to the unpleasant but necessary realities of life and work situations. The ability to think logically and to have a positive constructive

outlook on life and work without ignoring realities or responsibilities.

6. Communication - effective managers must recognize the need for two-way communication between themselves and their subordinates, and between themselves and their supervisors.
7. Objectivity - the ability to see that there are two or ten sides to every story is extremely important. Managers must be able to restrain and control their own emotional reactions. They must gather all facts, listen to all sides of the story, then reach a decision.
8. Social sensitivity - the caring manager must understand employees feelings and respond accordingly. Managers must be able to "put themselves into the shoes" of those who are under their direction.
9. Intelligence - the ability to think clearly is important. The manager has to understand management principles, put them to use, and direct subordinates capably.
10. Must demonstrate initiative and leadership qualities.
11. Should be innovative in developing workable schedules as the programs and policies evolve and change from season to season.
12. Exceptional interest and enthusiasm.
13. Ability to develop course outlines, evaluation of reports, inventories, requisitions, and budgets.
14. Excellent health and vitality.

Position Duties and Responsibilities

General Responsibilities

A. Areas of administration, public relations, and program as listed in the Annual Plan of Work, Science Program Director Notebook, and as assigned by the Director(s).

B. Administration of program and supervision of site as designated by the Director(s). (I.C.O.P. - In Charge Of Property)

C. To assure compliance with all standards and regulations for operations as legislated by local, state, and federal laws and/or agencies

D. Know and/or learn to be responsible for all areas of operation appropriate to the position held:

1. To be the representative of management - loyal to the management and equally loyal to employees;
2. To see that programs are well prepared, properly carried out and that their costs fall within budgetary limits;
3. To prepare time and work schedules for personnel, as assigned;
4. To balance the work load among assigned employees;
5. To keep job descriptions up to date;
6. To see that safety standards are observed; inform Director(s) or any infractions;
7. To instruct employees in the maintenance and care of equipment as appropriate to specific position;
8. To be responsible for maintaining good personal conduct and discipline; to be a positive influence on other staff;
9. To abide by and instruct all employees with regard to Seacamp/NHMI personnel practices and operating procedures, and enforce them when necessary;
10. As a member of the administrative staff, attend all administrative meetings and assist with planning, policy review/revision, etc.;

11. To make recommendations for improvements and to be a decision-maker within own area of responsibility;
12. To be responsible for keeping abreast of changes within the field, keeping up-to-date on new programs and techniques. Managers are actively involved in continuing their own education and striving to improve their managerial techniques. They are also responsible for the continuing education of employees they supervise, within the limitations of allocated resources.

E. Participate in all Seacamp/NHMI functions.

F. Review and update Plan of Work and Science Program Director Manual on an annual basis.

G. Write and submit monthly plans of work and monthly reports.

Specific Duties

A. Recruit and hire, following Sea camp procedures, a science program staff of 15+ instructors each season.

B. Supervise program specialist in production of science staff schedules.

C. Assist Director of Science Education with observation/critique of science program staff. Submit written evaluations to the Director(s) and review your evaluation with the instructors individually.

D. Assist Director of Science Education with updating of Habitat Resource Manual, staff training and program administration guidelines, as needed.

E. Supervise site visit logs by each instructor and supply copy to the Director(s).

F. Participate in orientation and training of science instructors, interns and assistants.

G. Assist with general staff training, as assigned.

H. Complete a preliminary budget for science program and review with the Director(s).

I. Participate in development of the annual report to Board of Directors.

J. Outline science procedures and regulations for staff and campers/students.

K. Update science curriculum files and science course outlines, as assigned.

L. Assist Director of Science Education to upgrade laboratory and library resources.

M. Report boat maintenance problems/needs to the Harbormaster.

N. Assist Waterfront Director approving staff boat requests, as needed.

O. Complete end of season report(s)/evaluation(s).

P. Hold monthly performance evaluation meetings with science instructors.

Q. Summer Camp:

1. Schedule guest speakers for summer science nights, assign valves for science activity night and at least one science valve for the other evening programs; supply calendars to Camp Director, Head Unit Leader, and the Scheduling Coordinator.
2. Outline a schedule of boat trips, van trips, and labs; supply a copy to the Waterfront Director, Scheduling Coordinator, Head Unit Leader, and Camp Directors.
3. Assist the SCUBA Director on selecting instructors for SCUBA science classes; and review camper requests before deciding on which and how many classes are to be offered. Review with the Camp Director before assigning staff to courses and schedules.
4. Supervise camper awards and participation certificates for science classes.

5. Give meal time announcements per week about what is happening in the science classes and/or program.
6. Produce and edit the Seacamp Journal of Marine Science.

Laboratory/Library Supervision

A. Maintain lab in good condition.

B. Maintain science program supply budget. Requisition supplies and materials; approve all purchases made by the science instructors.

C. Supervise inventory of laboratory stockroom and library.

D. Summer camp:

1. Have the lab cleaned and interest areas set up for Visitor's Day.
2. Supervise the lab campership.
3. Supervise the maintenance/storage of A.V. equipment in coordination with the staff photographer.

Teaching

A. Coordinate/Teach programs in tropical marine science for visiting advanced school groups, as assigned.

B. Instruct or assist in the science/SCUBA programs, as needed or as is desirable.

C. Coordinate any special science programs (i.e. thematic, International, Girl Scouts, Monroe County, etc.).

D. Maintain all school records, reports, etc. required of the position (see instructor/coordinator duties).

LEADERSHIP IN ORGANIZATIONS

Many people believe that leadership is simply being the first, biggest or most powerful. Leadership in organizations has a different and more meaningful definition. Very simply put, a leader is interpreted as someone who sets direction in an effort and influences people to follow that direction. How they set that direction and influence people depends on a variety of factors that we'll consider later on below. To really comprehend the "territory" of leadership, you should briefly scan some of the major theories, notice various styles of leadership and review some of the suggested traits and characteristics that leaders should have. The rest of this library should help you in this regard.

Theories About Leadership

There are also numerous theories about leadership, or about carrying out the role of leader, e.g., servant leader, democratic leader, principle-centered leader, group-man theory, great-man theory, traits theory, visionary leader, total leader, situational leader, etc.

New Paradigm in Management

Driving Forces of Change

Around the 1960s and on to today, the environment of today's organizations has changed a great deal. A variety of driving forces provoke this change. Increasing telecommunications has "shrunk" the world substantially. Increasing diversity of workers has brought in a wide array of differing values, perspectives and expectations among workers. Public consciousness has become much more sensitive and demanding that organizations be more socially responsible. Much of the third-world countries has joined the global marketplace, creating a wider arena for sales and services. Organizations became responsible not only to stockholders (those who owned stock) but to a wider community of "stakeholders."

As a result of the above driving forces, organizations were required to adopt a "new paradigm," or view on the world, to be more sensitive, flexible and adaptable to the demands and expectations of stakeholder demands. Many organizations have abandoned or are abandoning the traditional top-down, rigid and hierarchical structures to more "organic" and fluid forms.

Today's leaders and/or managers must deal with continual, rapid change. Managers faced with a major decision can no longer refer back to an earlier developed plan for direction. Management techniques must continually notice changes in the environment and organization, assess this change and manage change. Managing change does not mean controlling it, rather understanding it, adapting to it where necessary and guiding it when possible.

Managers can't know it all or reference resources for every situation. Managers must count on and listen more to their employees. Consequently, new forms of organizations are becoming more common, e.g., worker-centered teams, self-organizing and self-designing teams, etc.

Traits of the New Paradigm

Old Paradigm	New Paradigm
promote consumption at all costs	appropriate consumption
people to fit jobs	jobs to fit people
imposed goals, top-down decision making	autonomy encouraged, worker participation
fragmentation in work and roles	cross-fertilization by specialists seeing wide relevance
identification with job	identity transcends job description
clock model of company	recognition of uncertainty
aggression, competition	cooperation
work and play separate	blurring of work and play
manipulation and dominance	cooperation with nature
struggle for stability	sense of change, of becoming
quantitative	qualitative as well as quantitative
strictly economic motives	spiritual values transcend material gain
polarized	transcends polarities
short-sighted	ecologically sensitive
rational	rational and intuitive

emphasis on short-term solutions	recognition that long-range efficiency must take in to account harmonious work environment
centralized operations	decentralized operations when possible
runaway, unbridled technology	appropriate technology
allopathic treatment of symptoms	attempt to understand the whole, locate deep underlying causes of disharmony

Many people today are seeking to understand — and many people are writing about — the concept and practices of leadership. There are a great many reasons for the popularity of the topic, including that organizations are faced with changes like never before. The concept of leadership is relevant to any aspect of ensuring effectiveness in organizations and in managing change.

There has been an explosion of literature about leadership lately. Leading is a very human activity — we're all human — so there are many people who consider themselves experts on leadership. Unfortunately, many people make strong assertions about leadership without ever really understanding a great deal about leadership. Understanding the concept of leadership requires more than reading a few articles or fantasizing about what great leaders should be.

Great Confusion about the Term "Leadership" Today

Discussions about leadership today have become so frequent and impassioned, that they have become almost evangelical in tone. Leading is a very human activity — everyone's human — so everyone's got advice about leading. We associate any desirable trait to what leaders should be. People exhort others to become better leaders, to more effectively manage change, etc.

While this trend has reminded us of the critical importance of leadership and sometimes greatly inspired us on to greater achievements in life and work, it also has diffused the concept of leadership to the extent that the term has become almost useless in really helping people to become more effective in organizations.

Leadership Cube

Different people tend to talk about leadership from many different perspectives and not even realize that they are doing so. It is very simplistic to generalize about leadership as if the term applies the same way in every situation. Understanding the concept of leadership requires more than reading a few articles or fantasizing about what great leaders should be. To really understand leadership, one must understand "Leadership Cube." The Cube represents at least 20 different perspectives on leadership.

The Cube includes the following dimensions:

1) Five domains of leadership
2) Two contexts of leadership
3) Two orientations of leadership

Imagine each of these 3 dimensions along one side of a box, or cube. That would produce a cube with 20 smaller cells (5 times 2 times 2 = 20). Each of the 20 cells represents a unique perspective on leadership. You might consider some or all of the cells the next time that you use the term "leadership" in your studies, writings, research, discussions, etc.

Five Domains of Leadership

Domain	**Relevant Leadership Skills**
Leading yourself	Time management, stress management, assertiveness, etc.
Leading other individuals	Coaching, mentoring, delegating, etc.
Leading other groups	Meeting management, facilitation skills, etc.
Leading organizations	Strategic planning, Balanced Scorecard, etc.
Leading communities, societies, etc.	Community organizing, political skills, etc.

Two Contexts of Leadership

Context	Focus of Context
Roles	Board Chair, Chief Executive Officer, executive roles, etc.
Traits	Charismatic, influential, ethical, etc.

Two Orientations of Leadership

Orientation	Leadership Values
Results-oriented	Timeliness, efficiency, work direction, authority, etc.
Relationship-oriented	Participation, empowerment, relationships, etc.

Chapter 3

Leadership Trainning

The word leadership can refer to:

1. The process of leading
2. The concept of leading
3. Those entities that perform one or more acts of leading.

Terminology, Usage and Conceptual Scope

House defines "leadership" organizationally and narrowly as "the ability of an individual to influence, motivate, and enable others to contribute toward the effectiveness and success of the organizations of which they are members" (House, R. J. 2004: page 15). Compare the discussions on group leadership and *ad hoc* leadership below. One can also characterize leadership by the period of the authority, as in "During the 1940s Russia was under Stalinist leadership". In formal hierarchies the term can also serve to describe the position or relationships which allow and legitimize the exercising of what one might term "leadership behaviour".

In some languages the term for a leader and the term for the principle of leadership have very different meanings. Furthermore, note the different connotations of a synonym of the word "leader" adopted from the German: the word Führer, and its accompanying ideas on the Fuhrerprinzip.

It would-be controlling groups such as the military, political parties, ruling elites, and other belief-based enterprises like religions or businesses, the idea of leadership can become a Holy Grail and people can come to expect transformational change stemming from the leader; such entities may encourage their followers and believers to worship leadership, to respect it, and to strive (whether realistically or not) to become proficient in it. Ideally, one cannot buy or sell leadership in the military (or elsewhere); instead, leaders must ratify their position of command in the hearts and minds of their soldiers in order to obtain the best from them. Followers in such a situation may become uncritically obedient. Personal strategies that one can use to guard against the unrealistic expectations associated with belief in leaders include:

- Maintaining a questioning and skeptical attitude.
- Bolstering confidence in one's own decision-making abilities.

Categories and types of Leadership

One can categorize the exercise of leadership as either actual or potential:

- Actual - giving guidance or direction, as in the phrase "the emperor has provided satisfactory leadership"
- Potential - the capacity or ability to lead, as in the phrase "she could have exercised effective leadership"; or in the concept "born to lead".

Leadership can have a formal aspect (as in most political or business leadership) or an informal one (as in most friendships). Speaking of "leadership" (the abstract term) rather than of "leading" (the action) usually implies that the entities doing the leading have some "leadership skills" or competencies. Several types of entities may provide or exhibit leadership, actual or potential, including:

- A person in a position or office of authority, such as a President or a chairperson
- A person in a position or office associated with expertise, skill, or experience, such as a team leader, a ship's captain, a chief engineer, a chief, or a parent

- A group or person in the vanguard of some trend or movement, as in fashion trend-setters
- A group of respected people, (called a "reference group" by sociologists) such as business commentators or union spokespersons
- A product that influences other product offerings in a competitive marketplace

Leadership can come from an individual, a collective group of leaders, or even from the disincarnate — if not mystical — characteristics of a celebrity figurehead (compare hero). Yet other usages have a "leadership" which does little active leading, but to which followers show great (often traditional) respect (compare the courtesy title *reverend*). Followers often endow the leader with status or prestige. Aside from the prestige-role sometimes granted to inspirational leaders, a more mundane usage of the word "leadership" can designate current front-runners that exercise influence over competitors, for example, a corporation or a product can hold a position of "market leadership" without any implication of permanence or of merited respect.

Note that the ability to influence others does form an integral part of the "leadership" of some but not all front-runners. A front-runner in a sprint may "lead" the race, but does not have a position of "leadership" if he does not have the potential to influence others in some way. Thus one can make an important distinction between "being in the lead" and the process of leadership. Leadership implies a relationship of power — the power to guide others.

Leadership Associated with Positions of Authority

In On Heroes, Hero-Worship, and the Heroic in History, Thomas Carlyle demonstrated the concept of leadership associated with a position of authority (auctoritas in Latin). In praising Oliver Cromwell's use of power to bring King Charles I to trial and eventual beheading, he wrote the following: "Let us remark, meanwhile, how indispensable everywhere a King is, in all movements of men. It is strikingly shown, in this very War, what becomes of men when they cannot find a Chief Man, and their enemies can."

From this viewpoint, leadership emerges when an entity as "leader" contrives to receive deference from other entities who become "followers". And as the passage from Carlyle demonstrates, the process of getting deference can become competitive in that the emerging "leader" draws "followers" from the factions of the prior or alternative "leaders".

In representative democracies the people retain sovereignty (popular sovereignty) but delegate day-to-day administration and leadership to elected officials. In the United States, for example, the Constitution provides an example of recycling authority. In the Constitutional Convention of 1787, the American Founders rejected the idea of a monarch. But they still proposed leadership by people in positions of authority, with the authority split into three powers: in this case the legislative, the executive, and the judiciary. Under the American theory, the authority of the leadership derives from the power of the voters as conveyed through the electoral college. Many individuals share authority, including the many legislators in the Senate and the House of Representatives.

Leadership Cycles

If a group or an organization wants or expects identifiable leadership, it will require processes for appointing/acquiring and replacing leaders.

Traditional closed groups rely on bloodlines or seniority to select leaders and/or leadership candidates: monarchies, tribal chiefdoms, oligarchies and aristocratic societies rely on (and often define their institutions by) such methods.

Competence or perceived competence provides a possible basis for selecting leadership elites from a broader pool of potential talent. Political lobbying may prove necessary in electoral systems, but immediately demonstrated skill and character may secure leadership in smaller groups such as gangs.

Many organizations and groups aim to identify, foster and promote what they see as leadership potential or ability - especially among younger members of society..

The issues of succession planning or of legitimation become important at times when leadership (particularly individual leadership) might or must change due to term-expiry, accident or senescence.

Leadership as a Phase in Human Life-Cycles

Some cultures, especially those with a reverence for age and wisdom, see leadership as a standard part of the life-cycle of a person. Just as a youth becomes initiated into adulthood, so an adult may gain initiation as a leader. Such societies may require special reinforcement of the respect and kudos due to such senior members in order to maintain their position. If aged adults can no longer hunt or fight or play a full part in physical labor, for example, those adults' positions in society must rest on respect and implied wisdom and teaching roles, whether or not they show identified "leadership traits".

Titles emphasizing Authority

At certain stages in their development, the hierarchies of social ranks implied different degrees or ranks of leadership in society. Thus a knight led fewer men in general than did a duke; a baronet might in theory control less land than an earl. See peerage for a systematization of this hierarchy, and order of precedence for links to various systems.

In the course of the 19th and 20th centuries, several political operators took non-traditional paths to become dominant in their societies. They or their systems often expressed a belief in strong individual leadership, but existing titles and labels ("King", "Emperor", "President" and so on) often seemed inappropriate, insufficient or downright inaccurate in some circumstances. The formal or informal titles or descriptions they or their flunkeys employed express and foster a general veneration for leadership of the inspired and autocratic variety. The definite article when used as part of the title (in languages which use definite articles) emphasizes the existence of a sole "true" leader. Cases include:

- Caudillos in Spanish-speaking countries, notably Spain's Francisco Franco, Chile's Augusto Pinochet or the Dominican Republic's Rafael Trujillo
- Conducãtor in Romania - Nicolae Ceau°escu
- Il Duce in Italy - Benito Mussolini
- Der Fuhrer in Germany - Adolf Hitler
- The Dear Leader in North Korea - Kim Jong-il
- The Great Helmsman in China - Mao Zedong
- The Great Leader in North Korea - Kim Il-sung
- Vozd in Serbia - Karadjordje
- Poglavnik in Croatia - Ante Paveliæ
- Vozhd in the Soviet Union - Joseph Stalin

The different etymologies of these titles suggest various images of leadership: that of a "driver" (Führer, Vozhd), of a "head" (Caudillo, Poglavnik), or of someone followed (Duce, *Conducator*).

Such titles, and even the personal names associated with them, may also appear with reference — often jocular — to heirs and would-be imitators. Thus people may continue to speak of *little Hitlers* in a workplace or refer to a non-collegial prime minister ironically as *The Great Helmsman*. Compare the way in which the personal family name *Caesar* and the adopted by-name *Augustus* became effectively titles or designations for successive heads of the Roman Empire.

The whole structure of military hierarchies and the idea and the titles of an officer corps tend to reinforce the importance attached to leadership and to the chain of command in the military. Thus (for example) other ranks defer to Lieutenants who defer to Majors who defer to Colonels who defer to Generals who defer to Marshals. Similar elaborate structures of hierarchical leadership titles can occur in Christian churches (Deacon - Priest - Bishop - Archbishop - Cardinal) or in commercial enterprises (team leader - supervisor - line manager/middle manager - staff manager/ senior manager - vice president etc).

Informal, often spontaneously-generated titles or descriptions can provide informative insights. The use of "boss" in work-places and crime-syndicates may suggest a relatively loose hierarchy, while dubbing someone "chief" can express either instantaneous readiness to follow of an acknowledgment of collegiality.

Some titles can outstay their use. "Divine Augustus" fell prey to religious changes in the later Roman Empire. "Master" (or "Massa") has fallen out of general use in the American South, and "Baas" has new connotations in the new South Africa since the late 20th century.

Other honorifics can also change in accordance with social circumstances. Britons whose remote ancestors paid due deference to the local "lord" will now find that title more concentrated in the areas of politics and the law. Their American cousins have virtually confined the word "lord" to religious usage.

Symbolism of Leadership

Various symbolic attributes — often varying according to the cultural milieu — mark out authority-figures and help make them seem special and revered.

Leadership Amongst Primates

Richard Wrangham and Dale Peterson, in Demonic Males: Apes and the Origins of Human Violence present empirical evidence that only humans and chimpanzees, among all the animals living on earth, share a similar tendency for a cluster of behaviors: violence, territoriality, and competition for uniting behind the one chief male of the land. (Note the status of chimpanzees as humans' closest species-relatives: humans inherited 98% of their genes from the ancestors of the chimpanzees.

By comparison, bonobos, the second-closest species-relatives of man, do not unite behind the chief male of the land. The bonobos show deference to an alpha or top-ranking female that, with the support of her coalition of other females, can prove as strong as the strongest male in the land. Thus, if leadership amounts to getting the greatest number of followers, then among the bonobos, a female almost always exerts the strongest and most effective leadership.

Some have argued that, since the bonobo pattern inverts the dominant pattern among chimpanzees and men with regard to whether a female can get more followers than a male, humans and chimpanzees both likely inherited gender-bias against women from the ancestors of the chimpanzees; gender-bias features as a genetic condition of men. And the bias against women having leadership as a position of authority occurs in most cultures in the world. As of 2002, Sweden had the highest percentage of women in the legislature: but only 43%. And the United States, Andorra, Israel, Sierra Leone, and Ireland tied for 57th place with less than 15% of the legislature women. Admittedly, those percentages significantly outclass the occurrence of female chimpanzees becoming alpha of the community by getting the most followers, but similar trends exist in manifesting a general gender-bias across cultures against females gaining leadership as a position of authority over followers.

An alternative explanation suggests that those individuals best suited to lead e a group will somehow rise to the occasion and that followers (for some reason) will accept them as leaders or as proto-leaders. In this scenario, the traits of the leaders (such as gender, aggressiveness, etc.) will depend on the requirements of a given situation, and ongoing leadership may become extrapolated from a series of such situations.

In cultural anthropology, much speculation on the origins of human leadership relates to the perceived increasing need for dispute resolution in increasingly densely-populated and increasingly complex societies.

Leadership as a Vanguard

Sometimes followership can occur without intentional leadership. Despite (or because of) its mythical origin, the image of swarms of lemmings which follow the first lemming off a cliff appears frequently in characterizing followers. The animal kingdom also provides the actual model of the bellwether function in a mob of sheep. And human society also offers many examples of emulation. The fashion industry, for example, depends on it. Fashion marketers design clothing for celebrities, then offer less expensive variations/imitations for those who emulate the celebrities.

Another example of followership without intentional leadership comes with the market leadership of a pioneering company, or the price leadership of a monopolist. Other companies will emulate a successful strategy, product, or price, but originators may certainly not desire this - in fact they often do all they can legally do to prevent such direct competition.

The term "leadership" sometimes applies (confusingly) to a winning position in a race. One can speak of a front-runner in a sprint or of the "leader" in an election or poll as in a position of leadership. But such "leadership" does not involve any influence processes, and the "leader" will have followers who may not willingly choose to function as followers. Once again: one can make an important distinction between "in the lead" and the process of leadership. Once again, leadership implies a relationship of power - the power to guide others.

Leading from the front, in a military sense, may imply foolhardiness and unnecessary self-exposure to danger: these do not necessarily make for successful long-term leadership strategies.

Scope of Leadership

One can govern oneself, or one can govern the whole earth. In between, we may find leaders who operate primarily within:

- Families
- Bands
- Tribes
- States and nations
- Empires

Intertwined with such categories, and overlapping them, we find (for example) religious leaders (potentially with their own internal hierarchies), work-place leaders (executives, officers, senior/upper managers, middle managers, staff-managers, line-managers, team-leaders, supervisors) and leaders of voluntary associations.

Some anthropological ideas envisage a widespread (but by no means universal) pattern of progression in the organisation of society in ever-larger groups, with the needs and practices of leadership changing accordingly. Thus simple dispute resolution may become legalistic dispensation of justice before developing into proactive legislative activity. Some leadership careers parallel this sort of progression: today's school-board chairperson may become tomorrow's city councillor, then take in (say) a mayordom before graduating to nation-wide politics. Compare the *cursus honorum* in ancient Rome.

Orthogonality and Leadership

Those who sing the praises of leadership or of certain types of leadership may encounter problems in implementing consistent leadership structures. For example, a pyramidical structure in which authority consistently emanates from the summit can stifle initiative and leave no path for grooming future leaders in the ranks of subordinate levels. Similarly, a belief in universal direct democracy may become unwieldy, and a system consisting of nothing but representative leaders may well become stymied in committees.

Thus many leadership systems promote different rules for different levels of leadership. Hereditary autocrats meet in the United Nations on equal representative terms with elected governments in a collegial leadership. Or individual local democracies may assign some of their powers to temporary dictators in emergencies, as in ancient Rome. Hierarchies intermingle with equality of opportunity at different levels.

Support-Structures for Leadership

Though advocates of the "big man" school of visionary leadership would have us believe that charisma and personality alone can work miracles, most leaders operate within a structure of supporters and executive agents who carry out and monitor the expressed or filtered-down will of the leader. This undercutting of the importance of leadership may serve as a reminder of the existence of the follower: compare followership. A more or less formal bureaucracy (in the Weberian sense) can throw up a colorless nonentity as an entirely effective leader: this phenomenon may occur (for example) in a politburo environment. Bureaucratic organizations can also raise incompetent people to levels of leadership.

In modern dynamic environments formal bureaucratic organizations have started to become less common because of their inability to deal with fast-changing circumstances. Most modern business organizations (and some government departments) encourage what they see as "leadership skills" and reward identified potential leaders with promotions. According to B. Nanus, the forces that shape today's leading-edge organizations and their implications provide the key to visionary leadership.

To underline his point we can examine the success-story of Bill Gates: in brief he built Microsoft from the start as a twenty-first-century organization, and he allegedly runs it with a highly-developed sense of visionary leadership.

In a potential down-side to this sort of development, a big-picture grand-vision leader may foster another sort of hierarchy: a fetish of leadership amongst subordinate sub-leaders, encouraged to seize resources for their own sub-empires and to apply to the supreme leader only for ultimate arbitration.

Some leaders build coalitions and alliances: political parties abound with this type of leader. Still others depend on rapport with the masses: they labor on the shop-floor or stand in the front-line of battle, leading by example.

Determining What Makes "Effective Leadership"

In comparing various leadership styles in many cultures, academic studies have examined the patterns in which leadership emerges and then fades, sometimes by natural succession according to established rules and sometimes by the imposition of brute force.

The simplest way to measure the effectiveness of leadership involves evaluating the size of the following that the leader can muster. By this standard, Adolf Hitler became a very effective leader for a period — even if through delusional promises and coercive techniques. However, this approach may measure power rather than leadership. To measure leadership more specifically, one may assess the extent of influence on the followers, that is, the amount of leading. This may involve testing the results of leadership activities against a goal, vision, or objective.

James MacGregor Burns introduced a normative element: an effective Burnsian leader will unite followers in a shared vision that will improve an organization and society at large. Burns calls leadership that delivers "true" value, integrity, and trust transformational leadership. He distinguishes such leadership from "mere" transactional leadership that builds power by doing whatever will get more followers. But problems arise in quantifying the transformational quality of leadership - evaluation of that quality seems more difficult to quantify than merely counting the followers that the straw man of transactional leadership James MacGregor Burns has set as a primary standard for effectiveness. Thus transformational leadership requires an evaluation of quality, independent of the market demand that exhibits in the number of followers.

Current assessments of transformational and transactional leadership commonly make use of the Multifactor Leadership Questionnaire (MLQ), developed by Bass and Avolio in 1990. The MLQ measures four dimensions of transformational leadership:

1. Idealized influence
2. Inspirational motivation
3. Individualized consideration
4. Intellectual stimulation

The three dimensions of transactional leadership measured by the MLQ cover:

1. Contingent reward
2. Management by exception (active)
3. Management by exception (passive)

The functional leadership model conceives leadership as a set of behaviours that helps a group perform a task, reach their goal, or perform their function. In this model, effective leaders encourage functional behaviors and discourage dysfunctional ones.

In the path-goal model of leadership, developed jointly by Martin Evans and Robert House and based on the "Expectancy Theory of Motivation", a leader has the function of clearing the path toward the goal(s) of the group, by meeting the needs of subordinates.

Some commentators use the metaphor of an orchestral conductor to describe the quality of the leadership process. An effective leader resembles an orchestra conductor in some ways. He/she has to somehow get a group of potentially diverse and talented people - many of whom have strong personalities - to work together toward a common output. Will the conductor harness and blend all the gifts his or her players possess? Will the players accept the degree of creative expression they have? Will the audience enjoy the sound they make? The conductor may have a clear determining influence on all of these questions.

Suggested Qualities of Leadership

Studies of leadership have suggested qualities that people often associate with leadership. They include:

- Guiding others through modeling (in the sense of providing a role model) and through willingness to serve others first (compare followership)
- Talent and technical/specific skill at some task at hand
- Initiative and entrepreneurial drive

- Charismatic inspiration - attractiveness to others and the ability to leverage this esteem to motivate others
- Preoccupation with a role - a dedication that consumes much of leaders' life - service to a cause
- A clear sense of purpose (or mission) - clear goals - focus - commitment
- Results-orientation - directing every action towards a mission - prioritizing activities to spend time where results most accrue
- Optimism - very few pessimists become leaders
- Rejection of determinism - belief in one's ability to "make a difference"
- Ability to encourage and nurture those that report to them - delegate in such a way as people will grow
- Role models - leaders may adopt a *persona* that encapsulates their mission and lead by example
- Self-knowledge (in non-bureaucratic structures)
- Self-awareness - the ability to "lead" (as it were) one's own self prior to leading other selves similarly
- With regards to people and to projects, the ability to choose winners - recognizing that, unlike with skills, one cannot (in general) teach attitude. Note that "picking winners" ("choosing winners") carries implications of gamblers' luck as well as of the capacity to take risks, but "true" leaders, like gamblers but unlike "false" leaders, base their decisions on realistic insight (and usually on many other factors partially derived from "real" wisdom).
- Understanding what others say, rather than listening to how they say things - this could partly sum this quality up as "walking in someone else's shoes" (to use a common cliché).

The approach of listing leadership qualities, often termed "trait theory", assumes certain traits or characteristics will tend to lead to effective leadership. Although trait theory has an intuitive appeal, difficulties may arise in proving its tenets, and opponents frequently challenge this approach. The "strongest" versions of trait theory see these "leadership characteristics" as innate, and accordingly labels some people as "born leaders" due to their psychological makeup. On this reading of the theory, leadership development involves identifying and measuring leadership qualities, screening potential leaders from non-leaders, then training those with potential.

David McClelland, a Harvard-based researcher in the psychology of power and achievement, saw leadership skills, not so much as a set of traits, but as a pattern of motives. He claimed that successful leaders will tend to have a high need for power, a low need for affiliation, and a high level of what he called activity inhibition (one might call it self-control).

Situational leadership theory offers an alternative approach. It proceeds from the assumption that different situations call for different characteristics. According to this group of theories, no single optimal psychographic profile of a leader exists. The situational leadership model of Hersey and Blanchard, for example, suggest four leadership-styles and four levels of follower-development. For effectiveness, the model posits that the leadership-style must match the appropriate level of followership-development. In this model, leadership behaviour becomes a function not only of the characteristics of the leader, but of the characteristics of followers as well. Other situational leadership models introduce a variety of situational variables. These determinants include:

- The nature of the task (structured or routine)
- Organizational policies, climate, and culture
- The preferences of the leader's superiors
- The expectations of peers
- The reciprocal responses of followers

The contingency model of Vroom and Yetton uses other situational variables, including:

- The nature of the problem
- The requirements for accuracy
- The acceptance of an initiative
- Time-constraints
- Cost constraints

However one determines leadership behaviour, one can categorize it into various *leadership styles*. Many ways of doing this exist. For example, the Managerial Grid Model, a behavioral leadership-model developed by Robert Blake and Jane Mouton in 1964, suggests five different leadership styles, based on leaders' strength of concern for people and their concern for goal achievement.

Kurt Lewin, Ronald Lipitt, and R. K. White identified three leadership styles: authoritarian, democratic, and laissez-faire, based on the amount of influence and power exercised by the leader.

The Fiedler contingency model bases the leader's effectiveness on what Fred Fiedler called *situational contingency*. This results from the interaction of leadership style and situational favourableness (later called "situational control").

Leadership Styles

In 1994 House and Podsakoff attempted to summarize the behaviors and approaches of "outstanding leaders" that they obtained from some more modern theories and research findings. These leadership behaviors and approaches do not constitute specific styles, but cumulatively they probably characterize the most effective style of today's leaders/managers. The listed leadership "styles" cover:

1. Vision. Outstanding leaders articulate an ideological vision congruent with the deeply-held values of followers, a vision that describes a better future to which the followers have an alleged moral right.
2. Passion and self-sacrifice. Leaders display a passion for, and have a strong conviction of, what they regard as the moral correctness of their vision. They

engage in outstanding or extraordinary behavior and make extraordinary self-sacrifices in the interest of their vision and mission.

3. Confidence, determination, and persistence. Outstanding leaders display a high degree of faith in themselves and in the attainment of the vision they articulate. Theoretically, such leaders need to have a very high degree of self-confidence and moral conviction because their mission usually challenges the *status quo* and, therefore, may offend those who have a stake in preserving the established order.
4. Image-building. House and Podsakoff regard outstanding leaders as self-conscious about their own image. They recognize the desirability of followers perceiving them as competent, credible, and trustworthy.
5. Role-modeling. Leader-image-building sets the stage for effective role-modeling because followers identify with the values of role models whom they perceived in positive terms.
6. External representation. Outstanding leaders act as spokespersons for their respective organizations and symbolically represent those organizations to external constituencies.
7. Expectations of and confidence in followers. Outstanding leaders communicate expectations of high performance from their followers and strong confidence in their followers' ability to meet such expectations.
8. Selective motive-arousal. Outstanding leaders selectively arouse those motives of followers that the outstanding leaders see as of special relevance to the successful accomplishment of the vision and mission.
9. Frame alignment. To persuade followers to accept and implement change, outstanding leaders engage

in "frame alignment". This refers to the linkage of individual and leader interpretive orientations such that some set of followers' interests, values, and beliefs, as well as the leader's activities, goals, and ideology, becomes congruent and complementary.

10. Inspirational communication. Outstanding leaders often, but not always, communicate their message in an inspirational manner using vivid stories, slogans, symbols, and ceremonies.

Even though these ten leadership behaviors and approaches do not really equate to specific styles, evidence has started to accumulate that a leader's style can make a difference. Style becomes the key to the formulation and implementation of strategy and plays an important role in work-group members' activity and in team citizenship. Little doubt exists that the *way* (style) in which leaders influence work-group members can make a difference in their own and their people's performance.

Leadership and Vision

Many definitions of leadership involve an element of vision — except in cases of involuntary leadership and often in cases of traditional leadership. A vision provides direction to the influence process. A leader (or group of leaders) can have one or more visions of the future to aid them to move a group successfully towards this goal. A vision, for effectiveness, should allegedly:

- Appear as a simple, yet vibrant, image in the mind of the leader
- Describe a future state, credible and preferable to the present state
- Act as a bridge between the current state and a future optimum state
- Appear desirable enough to energize followers
- Succeed in speaking to followers at an emotional or spiritual level (logical appeals by themselves seldom muster a following)

For leadership to occur, according to this theory, some people ("leaders") must communicate the vision to others ("followers") in such a way that the followers adopt the vision as their own. Leaders must not just see the vision themselves, they must have the ability to get others to see it also. Numerous techniques aid in this process, including: narratives, metaphors, symbolic actions, leading by example, incentives, and penalties.

Stacey (1992) has suggested that the emphasis on vision puts an unrealistic burden on the leader. Such emphasis appears to perpetuate the myth that an organization must depend on a single, uncommonly talented individual to decide what to do. Stacey claims that this fosters a culture of dependency and conformity in which followers take no pro-active incentives and do not think independently.

LEADERSHIP'S RELATION WITH MANAGEMENT

Some commentators link leadership closely with the idea of management; some would even regard the two as synonymous. If one accepts this premise, one can view leadership as:

- Centralized or decentralized
- Broad or focused
- Decision-oriented or morale-centred
- Intrinsic or derived from some authority

Any of the bipolar labels traditionally ascribed to management style could also apply to leadership style. Hersey and Blanchard use this approach: they claim that management merely consists of leadership applied to business situations; or in other words: management forms a sub-set of the broader process of leadership. They put it this way: "Leadership occurs any time one attempts to influence the behavior of an individual or group, regardless of the reason. Management is a kind of leadership in which the achievement of organizational goals is paramount."

However, a clear distinction between management and leadership may nevertheless prove useful. This would allow for a reciprocal relationship between leadership and management, implying that an effective manager should possess leadership skills, and an effective leader should demonstrate management skills.

Abraham Zaleznik (1977), for example, delineated differences between leadership and management. He saw leaders as inspiring visionaries, concerned about substance; while managers he views as planners who have concerns with process. Warren Bennis (1989) further explicated a dichotomy between managers and leaders. He drew twelve distinctions between the two groups:

- Managers administer, leaders innovate
- Managers ask how and when, leaders ask what and why
- Managers focus on systems, leaders focus on people
- Managers do things right, leaders do the right things
- Managers maintain, leaders develop
- Managers rely on control, leaders inspire trust
- Managers have a short-term perspective, leaders have a longer-term perspective
- Managers accept the status-quo, leaders challenge the status-quo
- Managers have an eye on the bottom line, leaders have an eye on the horizon
- Managers imitate, leaders originate
- Managers emulate the classic good soldier, leaders are their own person
- Managers copy, leaders show originality

Paul Birch (1999) also sees a distinction between leadership and management. He observed that, as a broad generalization, managers concerned themselves with tasks while leaders concerned themselves with people. Birch does not suggest that leaders do not focus on "the task." Indeed, the things that characterise a great leader include the fact that they achieve. The difference lies in the leader realising that the achievement of the task comes about through the goodwill and support of others, while the manager may not.

This goodwill and support originates in the leader seeing people as people, not as another resource for deployment in support of "the task". The manager often has the role of organizing resources to get something done. People form one of these resources, and many of the worst managers treat people as just another interchangeable item. A leader has the role of causing others to follow a path he/she has laid out or a vision he/she has articulated in order to achieve a task. Often, people see the task as subordinate to the vision. For instance, an organization might have the overall task of generating profit, but a good leader may see profit as a by-product that flows from whatever aspect of their vision differentiates their company from the competition.

Leadership does not only manifest itself as purely a business phenomenon. Many people can think of an inspiring leader they have encountered who has nothing whatever to do with business: a politician, an officer in the armed forces, a Scout or Guide leader, a teacher, etc. Similarly, management does not occur only as a purely business phenomenon. Again, we can think of examples of people that we have met who fill the management niche in non-business organisations. Non-business organizations should find it easier to articulate a non-money-driven inspiring vision that will support true leadership. However, often this does not occur.

Differences in the mix of leadership and management can define various management styles. Some management styles tend to de-emphasize leadership. Included in this group one could include participatory management, democratic management, and collaborative management styles. Other management styles, such as authoritarian management, micro-management, and top-down management, depend more on a leader to provide direction. Note, however, that just because an organisation has no single leader giving it direction, does not mean it necessarily has weak leadership. In many cases group leadership (multiple leaders) can prove effective. Having a single leader (as in dictatorship) allows for quick and decisive decision-making when needed as well as when not needed. Group decision-making sometimes earns the derisive label "committee-itis" because of the longer times required to make decisions, but group leadership can bring more expertise, experience, and perspectives through a democratic process.

Patricia Pitcher (1994) has challenged the bifurcation into leaders and managers. She used a factor analysis technique on data collected over 8 years, and concluded that three types of leaders exist, each with very different psychological profiles. She characterises one group as imaginative, inspiring, visionary, entrepreneurial, intuitive, daring, and emotional, and calls them "artists". In a second grouping she places "craftsmen" as well-balanced, steady, reasonable, sensible, predictable, and trustworthy. Finally she identifies "technocrats" as cerebral, detail-oriented, fastidious, uncompromising, and hard-headed. She speculates that no one profile offers a preferred leadership style. She claims that if we want to build, we should find an "artist leader"; if we want to solidify our position, we should find a "craftsman leader"; and if we have an ugly job that needs to get done (like downsizing), we should find a "technocratic leader." Pitcher also observed that a balanced leader exhibiting all three sets of traits occurs extremely rarely: she found none in her study.

Leadership by a Group

In contrast to individual leadership, some organizations have adopted group leadership. In this situation, more than one person provides direction to the group as a whole. Some organizations have taken this approach in hopes of increasing creativity, reducing costs, or downsizing. Others may see the traditional leadership of a boss as costing too much in team performance. In some situations, the maintenance of the boss becomes too expensive - either by draining the resources of the group as a whole, or by impeding the creativity within the team, even unintentionally.

A common example of group leadership involves cross-functional teams. A team of people with diverse skills and from all parts of an organization assembles to lead a project. A team structure can involve sharing power equally on all issues, but more commonly uses *rotating leadership*. The team member(s) best able to handle any given phase of the project become(s) the temporary leader(s).

For example, the Orpheus orchestra has performed for over thirty years without a conductor — that is, without a sole leader. As a team of over 25 members, it has drawn discriminating audiences, and has produced over 60 recordings for Deutsche Grammophon in successful competition with other world-class orchestras.

Rather than an autocratic or charismatic conductor deciding the overall conception of a work and then dictating how each individual is to perform the individual tasks, the Orpheus team generally selects a different "core group" for each piece of music. The core group provides leadership in working out the details of the piece, and presents their ideas to the whole team. Members of the whole team then participate in refining the final conception, rehearsal, and product, including checking from various places in the auditorium how the sound balances and verifying the quality of the final recording.

At times the entire Orpheus team may follow a single leader, but whom the team follows rotates from task to task, depending on the capabilities of its members.

The orchestra has developed seminars and training sessions for adapting the Orpheus Process to business.

Co-Leadership

As a compromise between individual leadership and an open group, leadership structures of two or three people or entities occur commonly. Ancient Rome preferred two consuls to a single king, and the Roman Empire grew to accommodate two Emperors - those of the East and of the West - simultaneously. The Middle Ages saw leadership divided between the secular and spiritual realms - between Emperor and Pope. Some groups - often left-wing or Green in orientation - employ a co-leader structure today.

Triumvirates have long served to balance leadership ambitions - notably in Rome in the first century BC, but also as recently as in the Soviet Union troikas of the 20th century. Compare the separation of powers (legislative, judicial and executive) formalised (for example) in the constitution of the United States of America.

Divided Leadership

Whereas sometimes one can readily and definitively identify the locus of leadership, in other circumstances the situation remains obscured. Pre-modern Japan offers a classical example: the emperors provided symbolic and religious leadership, but the shoguns embodied virtually all political and administrative leadership.

Similar dichotomies appear in many places and in many periods. Any constitutional monarch has a potentially confusing relationship with the day-to-day leader (typically a prime minister) who remains (at least theoretically) subordinate - socially as well as politically. Regents may stand against monarchs (and their supporters) during the minority or absence of those monarchs. Heads of state may operate at cross-purposes with heads of government (see governmental co-habitation). Political leaders may or may not align closely with religious leaders. And in federal-type systems, regional leadership and its potentially different systems may cross swords with national leaders. Not to mention the potentially conflicting leadership manifestations of boards of directors and of Chief Executives.

Leader Relationships with Followers

Greiner's study of the language of U.S. Presidents examined the relationship between leader and followers and observed that changes have taken place in the presidential use of words that define the leader and the community as one. Modern US presidents have an observed tendency to make more use of inclusive words like *we, us* and *our* in their inaugural speeches. The use of inclusive words may suggest an effort by these democratically selected leaders to make the community work together to solve problems collectively.

Historical Views on Leadership

Aristocratic thinkers have postulated that leadership depends on one's blue blood or genes: monarchy takes an extreme view of the same idea, and may prop up its assertions against the claims of mere aristocrats by invoking divine sanction: see the divine right of kings. Contrariwise, more democratically-inclined theorists have pointed to examples of meritocratic leaders, such as the Napoleonic marshals profiting from careers open to talent.

In the autocratic/paternalistic strain of thought, traditionalists recall the role of leadership of the Roman pater familias. Feminist thinking, on the other hand, may damn such models as patriarchal and posit against them emotionally-attuned, responsive, and consensual empathetic guidance and matriarchies.

Comparable to the Roman tradition, the views of Confucianism on "right living" relate very much to the ideal of the (male) scholar-leader and his benevolent rule, buttressed by a tradition of filial piety.

Within the context of Islam, views on the nature, scope and inheritance of leadership have played a major role in shaping sects and their history. See caliphate.

In the 19th century, the elaboration of anarchist thought called the whole concept of leadership into question. (Note that the Oxford English Dictionary traces the word "leadership" in English only as far back as the 19th century.) One response to this denial of élitism came with Leninism, which demanded an élite group of disciplined cadres to act as the vanguard of a socialist revolution, bringing into existence the dictatorship of the proletariat.

Other historical views of leadership have addressed the seeming contrasts between secular and religious leadership.

The doctrines of Caesaro-papism have recurred and had their detractors over several centuries. Christian thinking on leadership has often emphasized stewardship of divinely-provided resources - human and material - and their deployment in accordance with a Divine plan. Compare servant leadership.

For a more general take on leadership in politics, compare the concept of the statesman.

Specific Theories of Leadership

Giorgio Agamben

In State of Exception (2005), Agamben reads Carl Schmitt's theory of sovereignty in the light of Walter Benjamin. Agamben traces Schmitt's definition of sovereignty as the power to decide the state of exception to the Roman concept of auctoritas - the power to declare justitium. Agamben writes:

"It is significative that modern specialists were so enclined to admit that auctoritas was inherent to the living person of the pater or the princeps. What was evidently an ideology or a fictio aiming to be the groundwork of auctoritas ' preeminence or, at least, specific rank compared to potestas thus became a figure of right's immanence to life. (...) Although it is evident that there can't be an eternal human type that would incarnate itself each time in Augustus, Napoleon, Hitler, but only more or less similar mechanisms {"dispositif", a term often used by Foucault} - the state of exception, justitium, the auctoritas principis, the Führertum - put in use in more or less different circumstances, in the 1930s - overall, but not only - in Germany, the power that Weber had defined as "charismatic" is related to the concept of auctoritas and elaborated in a Führertum doctrine as the original and personal power of a leader. In 1933, in a short article intending to define the fundamental concepts of national-socialism, Schmitt defines the Führung principal by the "root identity between the leader and his entourage" {"identité de souche entre le chef et son entourage"} (we shall note the use of Weberian concepts)."

James MacGregor Burns

James MacGregor Burns (1978, p. 2) wrote that a study of the definition of the word leadership revealed 130 definitions. However, several generally-accepted variations on the definition appear in the management and leadership literature.

Burns concluded by presenting five characteristics of leadership, namely:

1. Leadership is collective (p. 452). James Burns regards the notion of one-person leadership as "a contradiction in terms", because both leaders and followers must exist. Also, an organization may have multiple leaders all acting in consort with one another.
2. Leadership is dissension (p. 453). Burns claims that leadership coexists with dissent. Indeed, much of the growth of any organization centers on the management/leadership of dissent – except in times of war.
3. Leadership is causative (p. 454). True Burnsian leadership affects the motives of individuals and groups of peoples and alters the course of the organizational history. It causes positive change.
4. Leadership is morally purposeful (p. 455). Burns sees leadership as goal-oriented, with leaders and followers pointing the way to some future state of the organization with plans about how those goals might be met.
5. Transforming leadership is elevating (p. 455). Engagement between leaders and followers takes place on a moral – but not a moralistic - plane, as both leaders and followers rise to live more principled lives.

Ronald Heifetz

Ronald Heifetz (Heifetz 1994) described the difference between a descriptive view and a prescriptive view of leadership. A descriptive view describes leadership and how it occurs, and a prescriptive view suggests how it should occur. The notion of "adaptive work" forms a central concept of Heifetz's prescriptive view. Heifetz pointed out (p. 37) that people fail to adapt to new and unsettling situations through six avoidance mechanisms:

1. Blaming others
2. Finding scapegoats (to the extent that this differs from blaming)
3. Externalizing the enemy
4. Denying that a problem exists
5. Jumping to conclusions
6. Finding a distracting issue

In a prescriptive view, the leader would squarely face the problem and avoid the six surface-level solutions of the non-leader. A true leader would help a community face reality and deal with the issues: finding solutions where none previously existed. Using the 1950s television character, the Lone Ranger, as an example, we see the Ranger in a weekly episode, moving from frontier town to frontier town, discovering problems wherever he goes, fixing the problems and riding off into the sunset. In this metaphor, the Ranger fixes the symptom, but not the problem. A Lone Ranger non-leader would catch fish to feed the poor while a true leader would teach the poor how to catch fish and would motivate them to do so. The true leader finds a way to help the community engage the problem and collectively find a solution. For more detail, see Heifetz, R. (1994). Leadership without easy answers. Cambridge, MA: Harvard University Press.

George Terry

George Terry (Terry, G. 1960) has defined leadership as: "the activity of influencing people to strive willingly for group objectives". If we define leadership simply as "influencing others to some purpose" and we define followership as "becoming influenced by others to accept (willingly or un willingly) some purpose", then leadership and followership emerge as two sides of the same coin. In this scenario, leadership - whether successful or not - has not occurred until at least one follower joins in. Likewise, no followership exists without someone or something (not necessarily a leader) to follow. However, in this latter case, a "leader" need not exercise deliberate or even conscious leadership - that is, followers can follow someone who is not trying to lead. Some see "unconscious leadership" as a dubious concept, however. Many, using a different definition of leadership, would claim that it does not classify as leadership at all - simply because no deliberate intention to lead exists. Unconscious "leading by example" (as the phrase has it) may nevertheless exemplify such "leadership".

Conscious Leadership

Dr. James Farr (1918 - 2000) argued not for any one "correct leadership style" but for the style that each situation requires. Great leaders require the use of nearly every leadership style: one must apply the correct style to meet the situation. Farr terms this "Conscious Leadership".

"Conscious Leadership" consists of the art and science of leading change from a self-aware perspective, with clarity of purpose and an acute insight into others' perspectives and state of mind. This fully-aware state uniquely allows leaders to properly inspire motivation in others and to choose the most appropriate course of action both to solve pressing problems and to effectively achieve long-term organizational goals.

Futurist John Renesch has written extensively on conscious leadership, which he advocates for everyone — not only those in positions of authority or holding designated titles. As he wrote in early 2001:

Conscious leaders don't tolerate conditions or processes where people feel the need to compromise their values — to "sell their souls" for the task at hand. Conscious leadership includes conscious discernment, a principle that demands performance, integrity, competence and a noncalloused form of spiritual toughness. The conscious leader does not sit with his or her head in the clouds, dreaming of utopian schemes and professing New Age idealism. The conscious leader walks in the spiritual and physical domains concurrently, remaining simultaneously grounded and comfortable in both.

Renesch also writes about "The Conscious Organization" which he defines as "one which continually examines itself, committed to becoming as conscious as it can. In other words, it has very low tolerance for unconsciousness. It possesses the collective will to be vigilant, the collective commitment to continuous evolution, and the collective courage to act."

Alternatives to Leadership

Within groups, alternatives to the cult of leadership include using decision-making structures such as co-operative ventures, collegiality, consensus, anarchism and applied democracy. One can down play the ubiquitous idea of leadership by using structures such as information clearing houses or stressing functions such as administration. Note the different implications and connotations of the two phrases "coalition of the willing" and "US-led coalition".

MANAGEMENT BY OBJECTIVES (MBO)

What is MBO?

Management by objectives (MBO) is a systematic and organized approach that allows management to focus on achievable goals and to attain the best possible results from available resources. It aims to increase organizational performance by aligning goals and subordinate objectives throughout the organization. Ideally, employees get strong input to identify their objectives, time lines for completion, etc. MBO includes ongoing tracking and feedback in the process to reach objectives.

MBO was first outlined by Peter Drucker in 1954 in his book 'The Practice of Management'. In the 90s, Peter Drucker himself decreased the significance of this organization management method, when he said: "It's just another tool. It is not the great cure for management inefficiency... Management by Objectives works if you know the objectives, 90% of the time you don't."

Core Concepts

According to Drucker managers should "avoid the activity trap", getting so involved in their day to day activities that they forget their main purpose or objective. Instead of just a few top-managers, all managers should:

- Participate in the strategic planning process, in order to improve the implementability of the plan, and
- Implement a range of performance systems, designed to help the organization stay on the right track.

Managerial Focus

MBO managers focus on the result, not the activity. They delegate tasks by "negotiating a contract of goals" with their subordinates without dictating a detailed roadmap for implementation. MBO is about setting yourself objectives and then breaking these down into more specific goals or key results.

Main Principle

The principle behind MBO is to make sure that everybody within the organization has a clear understanding of the aims, or objectives, of that organization, as well as awareness of their own roles and responsibilities in achieving those aims. The complete MBO system is to get managers and empowered employees acting to implement and achieve their plans, which automatically achieve those of the organization.

Where to Use MBO

The MBO style is appropriate for knowledge-based enterprises when your staff is competent. It is appropriate in situations where you wish to build employees' management and self-leadership skills and tap their creativity, tacit knowledge and initiative. MBO is also used by chief executives of multinational corporations (MNCs) for their country managers abroad.

Setting Objectives

- In MBO systems, objectives are written down for each level of the organization, and individuals are given specific aims and targets. "The principle behind this is to ensure that people know what the organization is trying to achieve, what their part of the organization must do to meet those aims, and how, as individuals, they are expected to help. This presupposes that organization's programs and methods have been fully considered. If they have not, start by constructing team objectives and ask team members to share in the process."
- "The one thing an MBO system should provide is focus", says Andy Grove who ardently practiced MBO at Intel. So, have your objectives precise and keep their number small. Most people disobey this rule, try to focus on everything, and end up with no focus at all.
- For MBO to be effective, individual managers must understand the specific objectives of their job and how those objectives fit in with the overall company objectives set by the board of directors. "A manager's job should be based on a task to be performed in order to attain the company's objectives... the manager should be directed and controlled by the objectives of performance rather than by his boss."
- The managers of the various units or sub-units, or sections of an organization should know not only the objectives of their unit but should also actively participate in setting these objectives and make responsibility for them.
- The review mechanism enables leaders to measure the performance of their managers, especially in the key result areas: marketing; innovation; human organization; financial resources; physical resources; productivity; social responsibility; and profit requirements.

- However, in recent years opinion has moved away from the idea of placing managers into a formal, rigid system of objectives. Today, when maximum flexibility is essential, achieving the objective rightly is more important.

Balance Between Management and Employee Empowerment

The balance between management and employee empowerment has to be struck, not by thinkers, but by practicing managers.

Turning their aims into successful actions, forces managers to master five basic operations:

- Setting objectives,
- Organizing the group,
- Motivating and communicating,
- Measuring performance, and
- Developing people, including yourself

These MBO operations are all compatible with empowerment, if you follow the main principle of decentralization: telling people what is to be done, but letting them achieve it their own way. To make the principle work well, people need to be able to develop personally. Further, different people have different hierarchy of needs and, thus, need to be managed differently if they are to perform well and achieve their potential.

Empowerment recognizes "the demise" of the command-and-control system, but remains a term of power and rank. A manager should view members of his or her team much as a conductor regards the players in the orchestra, as individuals whose particular skills contribute to the success of the enterprise. While people are still subordinates, the superior is increasingly dependent on the subordinates for getting results in their area of responsibility, where they have the requisite knowledge. In turn, these subordinates depend on their superior for direction and "above all, to define what the 'score' if for the entire organization, that is, what are standards and values, performance and results."

Managing for Results

The only place where meaningful management results can be won is the outside world. Managing for results is expansion of MBO into the marketplace. It is the theory and practice of how to produce results on the outside, in the market and economy.

To achieve these results, you should develop a solid, sound, customer-focused, and entrepreneurial strategy, aimed at market leadership, based on innovation, and tightly focused on decisive opportunities.

Individual Responsibility

MBO creates a link between top management's strategic thinking and the strategy's implementation lower down. Responsibility for objectives is passed from the organization to its individual members. It is especially

Important for knowledge-based organizations where all members have to be able to control their own work by feeding back from their results to their objectives.

Management by objectives is achieved through self-control, the tool of effectiveness. Today the worker is a self-manager, whose decisions are of decisive importance for results.

In such an organization, management has to ask each employee three questions:

- What should we hold you accountable for?
- What information do you need?
- What information do you owe the rest of us?

The major outcome of strategic road-mapping and strategic planning, after gathering all necessary information, is the setting of goals for the organization based on its vision and mission statement. A goal is a long-range aim for a specific period. It must be specific and realistic. Long-range goals set through strategic planning are translated into activities that will ensure reaching the goal through operational planning.

Setting Objectives

- An objective is a specific step, a milestone, which enables you to accomplish a goal. Setting objectives involves a continuous process of research and decision-making. Knowledge of yourself and your unit is a vital starting point in setting objectives.
- Strategic planning takes place at the highest levels; other managers are involved with operational planning. The first step in operational planning is defining objectives - the result expected by the end of the budget (or other designated) cycle.
- Setting right objectives is critical for effective performance management. Such objectives as higher profits, shareholder value, customer sâtisfaction may be admirable, but they don't tell managers what to do. "They fail to specify priorities and focus. Such objectives don't map the journey ahead - the discovery of better value and solutions for the customer."

The objectives must be:

- Be focused on a result, not an activity
- Be consistent
- Be specific
- Be measurable
- Be related to time
- Be attainable
- Applying Feedback Analysis
- Undertake a feedback analysis to compare actual results with expectations. Whenever you take a decision or action, write down what you expect to happen. Review results at regular intervals, and compare them with expectations. Use this feedback analysis as a guide to reinforce strengths and eliminate weaknesses as well as for the next round of setting objectives.

Why Measure Performance?

The basic purpose of any measurement system is to provide feedback, relative to your goals, that increases your chances of achieving these goals efficiently and effectively. Measurement gains true value when used as the basis for timely decisions.

Measurement is Not an Essence, but Improvement

The purpose of measuring is not to know how your business is performing but to enable it to perform better. The ultimate aim of implementing a performance measurement system is to improve the performance of your organization. If you can get your performance measurement right, the data you generate will tell you where you are, how you are doing, and where you are going.

Modern Systems Approach

You must master your systems thinking skills as measurement today must be neither and end nor an activity in itself but a part of an integrated system for enhancing business performance. "A contemporary approach to measurement recognizes that modern business are complex systems, for which intuition no longer suffices. Today any action that a manager takes can have myriad and unpredictable consequences throughout the organization. Therefore measurement must be based on a careful through-through analysis of the business, one that links the objectives of the business to the things over which managers and front-line personnel have control. Only then can the recognition of a problematic measure lead to the right actions that will correct it and to improved performance of the business a whole".

Transforming the Traditional Functional Mindset

Traditional functional way of thinking "stands in the way of executives understanding and improving the flow of cross-functional activities which create enduring value for customers and shareholders. It encourages a distorted view of performance measurement and executive rewards, shifting focus away from meaningful measures such as the timeliness and quality of services provided to customers, and towards less significant measures around functional departmental performance."

Balanced Scorecard

The Balanced Scorecard is a framework for designing a set of measures for activities chosen by you as being the key drivers of your business. By having four distinct perspectives (financial, customer, internal process and innovation and learning) it promotes a more holistic view of the business.

Economic Value Added (EVA)

Economic Value Added (EVA), or economic rent, is a widely recognized tool that is used to measure the efficiency with which a company has used its resources. In other words, EVA is the difference between return achieved on resources invested and the cost of resources. Higher the EVA, better the level of resource unitization.

Measuring Cleaner Production

Measuring cleaner production (CP) is of critical importance. You must use appropriate indicators, which are generally applicable, yet specifically measurable, and address both the productivity and environmental aspects of your system in an integrated fashion. The indicators should enable not only estimation of the CP of a product or process and its comparison with other equivalents, but also improvement of the existing process or product and the development of new products.

Life Cycle Assessment (LCA) and Total Cost Assessment (TCA) are two types of CP indicators that help managers understand the practical implications of GP and make right decisions.

STAFF ATTITUDES

Maslow's Hierarchy of Needs

Maslow's Hierarchy of Needs is a theory in psychology that Abraham Maslow proposed in his 1943 paper A Theory of Human Motivation, which he subsequently extended. His theory contends that as humans meet 'basic needs', they seek to satisfy successively 'higher needs' that occupy a set hierarchy. Maslow studied exemplary people such as Albert Einstein, Jane Addams, Eleanor Roosevelt, and Frederick Douglass rather than mentally ill or neurotic people, writing that "the study of crippled, stunted, immature, and unhealthy specimens can yield only a cripple psychology and a cripple philosophy."

Maslow's hierarchy of needs is often depicted as a pyramid consisting of five levels: the four lower levels are grouped together as deficiency needs associated with physiological needs, while the top level is termed growth needs associated with psychological needs. While deficiency needs must be met, being needs are continually shaping behaviour. The basic concept is that the higher needs in this hierarchy only come into focus once all the needs that are lower down in the pyramid are mainly or entirely satisfied. Growth forces create upward movement in the hierarchy, whereas regressive forces push prepotent needs further down the hierarchy.

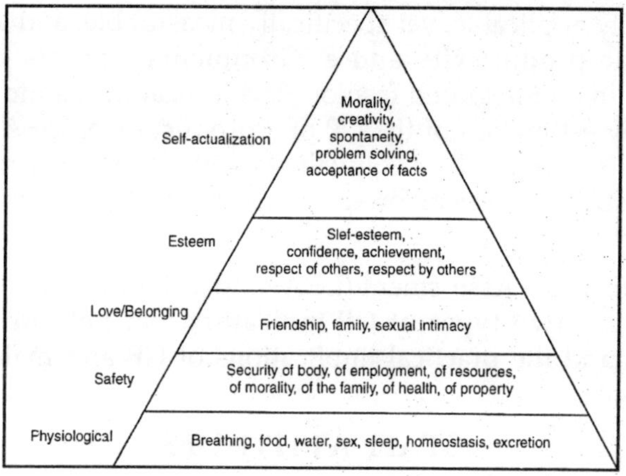

Deficiency Needs

The deficiency needs (also termed 'D-needs' by Maslow) are:

Physiological Needs

The physiological needs of the organism, those enabling homeostasis, take first precedence. These consist mainly of:

- The need to breathe
- The need to regulate homeostasis
- The need to eat
- The need to dispose of bodily wastes

If some needs are unmet, a human's physiological needs take the highest priority. As a result of the prepotency of physiological needs, an individual will deprioritize all other desires and capacities. Physiological needs can control thoughts and behaviours, and can cause people to feel sickness, pain, and discomfort.

Maslow also places sexual activity in this category, as well as bodily comfort, activity, exercise, etc. While several of these activities are important, many are not essential to survive.

Safety Needs

When physiological needs are met, the need for safety will emerge. Safety and security rank above all other desires. These include:

- Physical security - safety from violence, delinquency, aggressions
- Security of employment
- Security of revenues and resources
- Moral and physiological security
- Familial security
- Security of health
- Security of personal property against crime

A properly-functioning society tends to provide a degree of security to its members. Sometimes the desire for safety outweighs the requirement to satisfy physiological needs completely.

Love/Belonging Needs

After physiological and safety needs are fulfilled, the third layer of human needs is social. This involves emotionally-based relationships in general, such as:

- Friendship
- Sexual intimacy
- Having a supportive and communicative family

Humans generally need to feel belonging and acceptance, whether it comes from a large social group (clubs, office culture, religious groups, professional organizations, sports teams, gangs) or small social connections (family members, intimate partners, mentors, close colleagues, confidants). They need to love and be loved (sexually and non-sexually) by others. In the absence of these elements, many people become susceptible to loneliness, social anxiety, and depression. A lack of love and belonging is also beginning to be associated with physical illnesses such as heart disease (external source: heart disease).

Status (Esteem Needs)

According to Maslow, all humans have a need to be respected, to have self-respect, and to respect others. People need to engage themselves in order to gain recognition and have an activity or activities that give the person a sense of contribution and self-value, be it in a profession or hobby. Imbalances at this level can result in low self-esteem, inferiority complexes, an inflated sense of self-importance or snobbishness. There are two levels to Esteem needs. The lower of the levels relates to elements like fame, respect, and glory. The higher level is contingent to concepts like confidence, competence, and achievement. The lower level is generally considered poor. It is dependent upon other people, or someone who needs to be reassured because of lower esteem. People with low esteem need respect from others. They may seek fame or glory, which again are dependent on others. However confidence, competence and achievement only need one person and everyone else is inconsequential to one's own success.

Growth Needs

Though the deficiency needs may be seen as "basic", and can be met and neutralized (i.e. they stop being motivators in one's life), self-actualization and transcendence are "being" or "growth needs" (also termed "B-needs"), i.e. they are enduring motivations or drivers of behaviour.

Self-Actualization

Self-actualization (a term originated by Kurt Goldstein) is the *instinctual* need of humans to make the most of their unique abilities and to strive to be the best they can be. Maslow describes self-actualization as follows:

Self Actualization is the intrinsic growth of what is already in the organism, or more accurately, of what the organism is. (Psychological Review, 1949)

Maslow writes the following of self-actualizing people:

- They embrace the facts and realities of the world (including themselves) rather than denying or avoiding them.
- They are spontaneous in their ideas and actions.
- They are creative.
- They are interested in solving problems; this often includes the problems of others. Solving these problems is often a key focus in their lives.
- They feel a closeness to other people, and generally appreciate life.
- They have a system of morality that is fully internalized and independent of external authority.
- They judge others without prejudice, in a way that can be termed objective.

In short, self-actualization is reaching one's fullest potential.

Self-transcendence

At the top of the triangle, self-transcendence is also sometimes referred to as spiritual needs.

Viktor Frankl expresses the relationship between self-actualization and self-transcendence in Man's Search for Meaning. He writes:

> The true meaning of life is to be found in the world rather than within man or his own psyche, as though it were a closed system. Human experience is essentially self-transcendence rather than self-actualization. Self-actualization is not a possible aim at all, for the simple reason that the more a man would strive for it, the more he would miss it.... In other words, self-actualization cannot be attained if it is made an end in itself, but only as a side effect of self-transcendence. (p.175)

Maslow believes that we should study and cultivate peak experiences as a way of providing a route to achieve personal growth, integration, and fulfillment. Peak experiences are unifying, and ego-transcending, bringing a sense of purpose to the individual and a sense of integration. Individuals most likely to have peak experiences are self-actualized, mature, healthy, and self-fulfilled. All individuals are capable of peak experiences. Those who do not have them somehow depress or deny them.

Maslow originally found the occurrence of peak experiences in individuals who were self-actualized, but later found that peak experiences happened to non-actualizers as well but not as often. In his The Farther Reaches of Human Nature (New York, 1971) he writes:

> I have recently found it more and more useful to differentiate between two kinds of self-actualizing people, those who were clearly healthy, but with little or no experiences of transcendence, and those in whom transcendent experiencing was important and even central ... It is unfortunate that I can no longer be theoretically neat at this level. I find not only self-actualizing persons who transcend, but also nonhealthy people, non-self-actualizers who have important transcendent experiences. It seems to me that I have found some degree of transcendence in many people other than self-actualizing ones as I have defined this term.

Ken Wilber, a theorist and integral psychologist who was highly influenced by Maslow, later argued that a peak experience could occur at any stage of development and that "the way in which those states or realms are experienced and interpreted depends to some degree on the stage of development of the person having the peak experience." Wilber is in agreement with Maslow about the positive values of peak experiences saying, "In order for higher development to occur, those temporary states must become permanent traits." Wilber was, in his early career, a leader in Transpersonal psychology, a distinct school of psychology that is interested in studying human experiences which transcend the traditional boundaries of the ego.

In 1969, Abraham Maslow, Stanislav Grof and Anthony Sutich were the initiators behind the publication of the first issue of the Journal of Transpersonal Psychology.

Counterpositions

While Maslow's theory was regarded as an improvement over previous theories of personality and motivation, it has its detractors. For example, in their extensive review of research that is dependent on Maslow's theory, Wahba and Bridwell (1976) found little evidence for the ranking of needs that Maslow described, or even for the existence of a definite hierarchy at all. For example, less individualistic forms of society than described by Maslow in this theory, might value their social relationships (e.g. family, clan or group) higher than their own physiological needs.

The concept of self-actualization is considered vague and psychobabble by some behaviourist psychologists. The concept is based on an Aristotelian notion of human nature that assumes we have an optimum role or purpose. Self actualization is a difficult construct for researchers to operationalize, and this in turn makes it difficult to test Maslow's theory. Even if self-actualization is a useful concept, there is no proof that every individual has this capacity or even the goal to achieve it.

Other counterpositions suggest that not everyone ultimately seeks the self-actualization that a strict (and possibly naive) reading of Maslow's hierarchy of needs appears to imply:

- Viktor Frankl's book Man's Search for Meaning describes his psychotherapeutic method (logotherapy) of finding purpose in life.
- Albert Einstein was actually drawn toward the sense of mystery in life.
- Others seek to perform good works.
- Others are drawn toward the dark side of the human condition.

One could counter this argument by citing these as examples of ways people self-actualize. Hence, the ambiguity of the term.

Transcendence has been discounted by secular psychologists because they feel it belongs to the domain of religious belief. But Maslow himself believed that science and religion were both too narrowly conceived, too dichotomized, and too separated from each other. Non-peakers, as he would call them, characteristically think in logical, rational terms and look down on extreme spirituality as "insanity" (p. 22) because it entails a loss of control and deviation from what is socially acceptable. They may even try to avoid such experiences because they are not materially productive—they "earn no money, bake no bread, and chop no wood" (p. 23). Other non-peakers have the problem of immaturity in spiritual matters, and hence tend to view holy rituals and events in their most crude, external form, not appreciating them for any underlying spiritual implications. Maslow despised such people because they form a sort of idolatry that hinders religions (p. 24). This creates a divide in every religion and social institution. (Maslow. "The 'Core-Religious' or 'Transcendent,' Experience.") It is important to note, however, that Maslow considered himself to be an atheist—thus, by his conceptualization of transcendence, any individual can have such experiences (Hoffman, E. 1999.

In Mao's era (1893-1976), national unity and loyalty were not compromised in China. All farms were communal and no individual farming was allowed; industry was state-owned and operated; revolutionary pattern was recycled to attack societal classes taking form and keep China as classless as possible; lack of color in clothing was a hint of desensualization; groups were extensively used to control political, factory and commune work. Their group-oriented life style was also marked in the social life which centered on work unit activities and coworker lives as they all lived in the same apartment buildings. Once a Chinese individual belonged to a work unit, "iron rice bowl", like "golden handcuffs" in the U.S., was guaranteed with many basic needs cared for by the work unit and the government, such as housing, education and medical care.

This juxtaposition of belongingness and the satisfaction of the physical rewards resulted in the Chinese basic assumption of collectivism that being a good member of society and putting group goals before individual needs should govern all practices. Some other assumptions were national loyalty, equal pay and equal bonus regardless of skill or output differences, avoidance of personal credit for accomplishment, importance of communal property, and emphasis on group forces for motivation. On the contrary, Maslow's formulation was clearly made from basic American cultural assumptions stressing self-concept of individuals and individual achievement.

Moreover, ego needs and needs for self-actualization were not highly valued in Chinese culture in the way that Americans held it. Many Western observers noted the embarrassment of Chinese people at being singled out for individual achievements, and the fear being seen as special, or having more than the neighbors. Judging by his survey results from Chinese workers and graduate students, Nevis found that although social needs predominated over individual needs in China, what was worth speculating was that the difference between workers' and graduate students' survey ranks indicated that ego or self-esteem, which was missing in the

Chinese hierarchy and defined through items like "interesting job" and "full appreciation for work done", might emerge as a new level in the new generation of Chinese with the opening up of individual freedom in the country. Although actualization remained at the top of both hierarchies, to call the highest Chinese order of need "social confluence" might be more appropriate since self-actualization was understandable only in terms of contribution to society. However, American people perceive self-esteem needs as a driving force, and symbols of achievement as rewards for successful self-actualization.

Theory of Human Motivation

In a previous paper various propositions were presented which would have to be included in any theory of human motivation that could lay claim to being definitive. These conclusions may be briefly summarized as follows:

1. The integrated wholeness of the organism must be one of the foundation stones of motivation theory.
2. The hunger drive (or any other physiological drive) was rejected as a centering point or model for a definitive theory of motivation. Any drive that is somatically based and localizable was shown to be atypical rather than typical in human motivation.
3. Such a theory should stress and center itself upon ultimate or basic goals rather than partial or superficial ones, upon ends rather than means to these ends. Such a stress would imply a more central place for unconscious than for conscious motivations.
4. There are usually available various cultural paths to the same goal. Therefore conscious, specific, local-cultural desires are not as fundamental in motivation theory as the more basic, unconscious goals.
5. Any motivated behavior, either preparatory or consummatory, must be understood to be a channel

through which many basic needs may be simultaneously expressed or satisfied. Typically an act has more than one motivation.

6. Practically all organismic states are to be understood as motivated and as motivating.
7. Human needs arrange themselves in hierarchies of pre-potency. That is to say, the appearance of one need usually rests on the prior satisfaction of another, more pre-potent need. Man is a perpetually wanting animal. Also no need or drive can be treated as if it were isolated or discrete; every drive is related to the state of satisfaction or dissatisfaction of other drives.
8. *Lists* of drives will get us nowhere for various theoretical and practical reasons. Furthermore any classification of motivations must deal with the problem of levels of specificity or generalization the motives to be classified.
9. Classifications of motivations must be based upon goals rather than upon instigating drives or motivated behaviour.
10. Motivation theory should be human-centered rather than animal-centered.
11. The situation or the field in which the organism reacts must be taken into account but the field alone can rarely serve as an exclusive explanation for behavior. Furthermore the field itself must be interpreted in terms of the organism. Field theory cannot be a substitute for motivation theory.
12. Not only the integration of the organism must be taken into account, but also the possibility of isolated, specific, partial or segmental reactions. It has since become necessary to add to these another affirmation.
13. Motivation theory is not synonymous with behavior theory. The motivations are only one class of

determinants of behavior. While behavior is almost always motivated, it is also almost always biologically, culturally and situationally determined as well.

This is an attempt to formulate a positive theory of motivation which will satisfy these theoretical demands and at the same time conform to the known facts, clinical and observational as well as experimental. It derives most directly, however, from clinical experience. This theory is in the functionalist tradition of James and Dewey, and is fused with the holism of Wertheimer, Goldstein, and Gestalt Psychology, and with the dynamicism of Freud and Adler. This fusion or synthesis may arbitrarily be called a 'general-dynamic' theory.

It is far easier to perceive and to criticize the aspects in motivation theory than to remedy them. Mostly this is because of the very serious lack of sound data in this area. I conceive this lack of sound facts to be due primarily to the absence of a valid theory of motivation. The present theory then must be considered to be a suggested program or framework for future research and must stand or fall, not so much on facts available or evidence presented, as upon researches to be done, researches suggested perhaps, by the questions raised in this paper.

The Basic Needs

The 'physiological' needs. — The needs that are usually taken as the starting point for motivation theory are the so-called physiological drives. Two recent lines of research make it necessary to revise our customary notions about these needs, first, the development of the concept of homeostasis, and second, the finding that appetites (preferential choices among foods) are a fairly efficient indication of actual needs or lacks in the body.

Homeostasis refers to the body's automatic efforts to maintain a constant, normal state of the blood stream. Cannon (2) has described this process for (1) the water content of the blood, (2) salt content, (3) sugar content, (4) protein content,

(5) fat content, (6) calcium content, (7) oxygen content, (8) constant hydrogen-ion level (acid-base balance) and (9) constant temperature of the blood. Obviously this list can be extended to include other minerals, the hormones, vitamins, etc.

Young in a recent article has summarized the work on appetite in its relation to body needs. If the body lacks some chemical, the individual will tend to develop a specific appetite or partial hunger for that food element.

Thus it seems impossible as well as useless to make any list of fundamental physiological needs for they can come to almost any number one might wish, depending on the degree of specificity of description. We can not identify all physiological needs as homeostatic. That sexual desire, sleepiness, sheer activity and maternal behaviour in animals, are homeostatic, has not yet been demonstrated. Furthermore, this list would not include the various sensory pleasures (tastes, smells, tickling, stroking) which are probably physiological and which may become the goals of motivated behaviour.

In a previous paper it has been pointed out that these physiological drives or needs are to be considered unusual rather than typical because they are isolable, and because they are localizable somatically. That is to say, they are relatively independent of each other, of other motivations [p. 373] and of the organism as a whole, and secondly, in many cases, it is possible to demonstrate a localized, underlying somatic base for the drive. This is true less generally than has been thought (exceptions are fatigue, sleepiness, maternal responses) but it is still true in the classic instances of hunger, sex, and thirst.

It should be pointed out again that any of the physiological needs and the consummatory behavior involved with them serve as channels for all sorts of other needs as well. That is to say, the person who thinks he is hungry may actually be seeking more for comfort, or dependence, than for vitamins or proteins. Conversely, it is possible to satisfy the hunger need in part by other activities such as drinking water or smoking cigarettes. In other words, relatively isolable as these physiological needs are, they are not completely so.

Undoubtedly these physiological needs are the most pre-potent of all needs. What this means specifically is, that in the human being who is missing everything in life in an extreme fashion, it is most likely that the major motivation would be the physiological needs rather than any others. A person who is lacking food, safety, love, and esteem would most probably hunger for food more strongly than for anything else.

If all the needs are unsatisfied, and the organism is then dominated by the physiological needs, all other needs may become simply non-existent or be pushed into the background. It is then fair to characterize the whole organism by saying simply that it is hungry, for consciousness is almost completely preempted by hunger. All capacities are put into the service of hunger-satisfaction, and the organization of these capacities is almost entirely determined by the one purpose of satisfying hunger. The receptors and effectors, the intelligence, memory, habits, all may now be defined simply as hunger-gratifying tools. Capacities that are not useful for this purpose lie dormant, or are pushed into the background. The urge to write poetry, the desire to acquire an automobile, the interest in American history, the desire for a new pair of shoes are, in the extreme case, forgotten or become of sec-[p.374] importance. For the man who is extremely and dangerously hungry, no other interests exist but food.

He dreams food, he remembers food, he thinks about food, he emotes only about food, he perceives only food and he wants only food. The more subtle determinants that ordinarily fuse with the physiological drives in organizing even feeding, drinking or sexual behavior, may now be so completely overwhelmed as to allow us to speak at this time (but only at this time) of pure hunger drive and behavior, with the one unqualified aim of relief.

Another peculiar characteristic of the human organism when it is dominated by a certain need is that the whole philosophy of the future tends also to change. For our chronically and extremely hungry man, Utopia can be defined very simply as a place where there is plenty of food. He tends to think that, if only he is guaranteed food for the rest of his life, he will be perfectly happy and will never want anything more. Life itself tends to be defined in terms of eating. Anything else will be defined as unimportant. Freedom, love, community feeling, respect, philosophy, may all be waved aside as fripperies which are useless since they fail to fill the stomach. Such a man may fairly be said to live by bread alone.

It cannot possibly be denied that such things are true but their generality can be denied. Emergency conditions are, almost by definition, rare in the normally functioning peaceful society. That this truism can be forgotten is due mainly to two reasons. First, rats have few motivations other than physiological ones, and since so much of the research upon motivation has been made with these animals, it is easy to carry the rat-picture over to the human being. Secondly, it is too often not realized that culture itself is an adaptive tool, one of whose main functions is to make the physiological emergencies come less and less often. In most of the known societies, chronic extreme hunger of the emergency type is rare, rather than common. In any case, this is still true in the United States. The average American citizen is experiencing appetite rather than hunger when he says "I am [p. 375] hungry." He is apt to experience sheer life-and-death hunger only by accident and then only a few times through his entire life.

Obviously a good way to obscure the 'higher' motivations, and to get a lopsided view of human capacities and human nature, is to make the organism extremely and chronically hungry or thirsty. Anyone who attempts to make an emergency picture into a typical one, and who will measure all of man's goals and desires by his behaviour during extreme physiological deprivation is certainly being blind to many things. It is quite true that man lives by bread alone — when there is no bread. But what happens to man's desires when there is plenty of bread and when his belly is chronically filled?

At once other (and 'higher') needs emerge and these, rather than physiological hungers, dominate the organism. And when these in turn are satisfied, again new (and still 'higher') needs emerge and so on. This is what we mean by saying that the basic human needs are organized into a hierarchy of relative prepotency.

One main implication of this phrasing is that gratification becomes as important a concept as deprivation in motivation theory, for it releases the organism from the domination of a relatively more physiological need, permitting thereby the emergence of other more social goals. The physiological needs, along with their partial goals, when chronically gratified cease to exist as active determinants or organizers of behavior. They now exist only in a potential fashion in the sense that they may emerge again to dominate the organism if they are thwarted. But a want that is satisfied is no longer a want. The organism is dominated and its behavior organized only by unsatisfied needs. If hunger is satisfied, it becomes unimportant in the current dynamics of the individual.

This statement is somewhat qualified by a hypothesis to be discussed more fully later, namely that it is precisely those individuals in whom a certain need has always been satisfied who are best equipped to tolerate deprivation of that need in the future, and that furthermore, those who have been deprived in the past will react differently to current satisfactions than the one who has never been deprived.

The safety needs — If the physiological needs are relatively well gratified, there then emerges a new set of needs, which we may categorize roughly as the safety needs. All that has been said of the physiological needs is equally true, although in lesser degree, of these desires. The organism may equally well be wholly dominated by them. They may serve as the almost exclusive organizers of behavior, recruiting all the capacities of the organism in their service, and we may then fairly describe the whole organism as a safety-seeking mechanism. Again we may say of the receptors, the effectors, of the intellect and the other capacities that they are primarily safety-seeking tools. Again, as in the hungry man, we find that the dominating goal is a strong determinant not only of his current world-outlook and philosophy but also of his philosophy of the future. Practically everything looks less important than safety, (even sometimes the physiological needs which being satisfied, are now underestimated). A man, in this state, if it is extreme enough and chronic enough, may be characterized as living almost for safety alone.

Although in this paper we are interested primarily in the needs of the adult, we can approach an understanding of his safety needs perhaps more efficiently by observation of infants and children, in whom these needs are much more simple and obvious. One reason for the clearer appearance of the threat or danger reaction in infants, is that they do not inhibit this reaction at all, whereas adults in our society have been taught to inhibit it at all costs. Thus even when adults do feel their safety to be threatened we may not be able to see this on the surface. Infants will react in a total fashion and as if they were endangered, if they are disturbed or dropped suddenly, startled by loud noises, flashing light, or other unusual sensory stimulation, by rough handling, by general loss of support in the mother's arms, or by inadequate support

In infants we can also see a much more direct reaction to bodily illnesses of various kinds. Sometimes these illnesses seem to be immediately and *per se* threatening and seem to make the child feel unsafe. For instance, vomiting, colic or other sharp pains seem to make the child look at the whole world in a different way. At such a moment of pain, it may be postulated that, for the child, the appearance of the whole world suddenly changes from sunniness to darkness, so to speak, and becomes a place in which anything at all might happen, in which previously stable things have suddenly become unstable. Thus a child who because of some bad food is taken ill may, for a day or two, develop fear, nightmares, and a need for protection and reassurance never seen in him before his illness.

Another indication of the child's need for safety is his preference for some kind of undisrupted routine or rhythm.

He seems to want a predictable, orderly world. For instance, injustice, unfairness, or inconsistency in the parents seems to make a child feel anxious and unsafe. This attitude may be not so much because of the injustice *per se* or any particular pains involved, but rather because this treatment threatens to make the world look unreliable, or unsafe, or unpredictable. Young children seem to thrive better under a system which has at least a skeletal outline of rigidity, in which there is a schedule of a kind, some sort of routine, something that can be counted upon, not only for the present but also far into the future. Perhaps one could express this more accurately by saying that the child needs an organized world rather than an unorganized or unstructured one.

The central role of the parents and the normal family setup are indisputable. Quarreling, physical assault, separation, divorce or death within the family may be particularly terrifying. Also parental outbursts of rage or threats of punishment directed to the child, calling him names, speaking to him harshly, shaking him, handling him roughly, or actual physical punishment sometimes elicit such total panic and terror in the child that we must assume more is involved than the physical pain alone. While it is true that in some children this terror may represent also a fear of loss of parental love, it can also occur in completely rejected children, who seem to cling to the hating parents more for sheer safety and protection than because of hope of love.

Confronting the average child with new, unfamiliar, strange, unmanageable stimuli or situations will too frequently elicit the danger or terror reaction, as for example, getting lost or even being separated from the parents for a short time, being confronted with new faces, new situations or new tasks, the sight of strange, unfamiliar or uncontrollable objects, illness or death. Particularly at such times, the child's frantic clinging to his parents is eloquent testimony to their role as protectors (quite apart from their roles as food-givers and love-givers).

From these and similar observations, we may generalize and say that the average child in our society generally prefers a safe, orderly, predictable, organized world, which he can count, on, and in which unexpected, unmanageable or other dangerous things do not happen, and in which, in any case, he has all-powerful parents who protect and shield him from harm.

That these reactions may so easily be observed in children is in a way a proof of the fact that children in our society feel too unsafe (or, in a word, are badly brought up). Children who are reared in an unthreatening, loving family do not ordinarily react as we have described above. In such children the danger reactions are apt to come mostly to objects or situations that adults too would consider dangerous.

The healthy, normal, fortunate adult in our culture is largely satisfied in his safety needs. The peaceful, smoothly running, 'good' society ordinarily makes its members feel safe enough from wild animals, extremes of temperature, criminals, assault and murder, tyranny, etc. Therefore, in a very real sense, he no longer has any safety needs as active motivators. Just as a sated man no longer feels hungry, a safe man no longer feels endangered. If we wish to see these needs directly and clearly we must turn to neurotic or near-neurotic individuals, and to the economic and social underdogs. In between these extremes, we can perceive the expressions of safety needs only in such phenomena as, for instance, the common preference for a job with tenure and protection, the desire for a savings account, and for insurance of various kinds (medical, dental, unemployment, disability, old age).

Other broader aspects of the attempt to seek safety and stability in the world are seen in the very common preference for familiar rather than unfamiliar things, or for the known rather than the unknown. The tendency to have some religion or world-philosophy that organizes the universe and the men in it into some sort of satisfactorily coherent, meaningful whole is also in part motivated by safety-seeking. Here too we may list science and philosophy in general as partially motivated by the safety needs (we shall see later that there are also other motivations to scientific, philosophical or religious endeavor).

Otherwise the need for safety is seen as an active and dominant mobilizer of the organism's resources only in emergencies, *e. g.*, war, disease, natural catastrophes, crime waves, societal disorganization, neurosis, brain injury, chronically bad situation.

Some neurotic adults in our society are, in many ways, like the unsafe child in their desire for safety, although in the former it takes on a somewhat special appearance. Their reaction is often to unknown, psychological dangers in a world that is perceived to be hostile, overwhelming and threatening. Such a person behaves as if a great catastrophe were almost always impending, i.e., he is usually responding as if to an emergency. His safety needs often find specific expression in a search for a protector, or a stronger person on whom he may depend, or perhaps, a Fuehrer.

The neurotic individual may be described in a slightly different way with some usefulness as a grown-up person who retains his childish attitudes toward the world. That is to say, a neurotic adult may be said to behave 'as if' he were actually afraid of a spanking, or of his mother's disapproval, or of being abandoned by his parents, or having his food taken away from him. It is as if his childish attitudes of fear and threat reaction to a dangerous world had gone underground, and untouched by the growing up and learning processes, were now ready to be called out by any stimulus that would make a child feel endangered and threatened.

The neurosis in which the search for safety takes its dearest form is in the compulsive-obsessive neurosis. Compulsive-obsessives try frantically to order and stabilize the world so that no unmanageable, unexpected or unfamiliar dangers will ever appear; They hedge themselves about with all sorts of ceremonials, rules and formulas so that every possible contingency may be provided for and so that no new contingencies may appear. They are much like the brain injured cases, described by Goldstein, who manage to maintain their equilibrium by avoiding everything unfamiliar and strange and by ordering their restricted world in such a neat, disciplined, orderly fashion that everything in the world can be counted upon. They try to arrange the world so that anything unexpected (dangers) cannot possibly occur. If, through no fault of their own, something unexpected does occur, they go into a panic reaction as if this unexpected occurrence constituted a grave danger. What we can see only as a none-too-strong preference in the healthy person, *e. g.*, preference for the familiar, becomes a life-and-death necessity in abnormal cases.

The love needs — If both the physiological and the safety needs are fairly well gratified, then there will emerge the love and affection and belongingness needs, and the whole cycle already described will repeat itself with this new center. Now the person will feel keenly, as never before, the absence of friends, or a sweetheart, or a wife, or children. He will hunger for affectionate relations with people in general, namely, for a place in his group, and he will strive with great intensity to achieve this goal. He will want to attain such a place more than anything else in the world and may even forget that once, when he was hungry, he sneered at love.

In our society the thwarting of these needs is the most commonly found core in cases of maladjustment and more severe psychopathology. Love and affection, as well as their possible expression in sexuality, are generally looked upon with ambivalence and are customarily hedged about with many restrictions and inhibitions. Practically all theorists of psychopathology have stressed thwarting of the love needs as basic in the picture of maladjustment. Many clinical studies have therefore been made of this need and we know more about it perhaps than any of the other needs except the physiological ones.

One thing that must be stressed at this point is that love is not synonymous with sex. Sex may be studied as a purely physiological need. Ordinarily sexual behavior is multi-determined, that is to say, determined not only by sexual but also by other needs, chief among which are the love and affection needs. Also not to be overlooked is the fact that the love needs involve both giving *and* receiving love.

The Esteem needs — All people in our society (with a few pathological exceptions) have a need or desire for a stable, firmly based, (usually) high evaluation of themselves, for self-respect, or self-esteem, and for the esteem of others. By firmly based self-esteem, we mean that which is soundly based upon real capacity, achievement and respect from others. These needs may be classified into two subsidiary sets. These are, first, the desire for strength, for achievement, for adequacy, for confidence in the face of the world, and for independence and freedom. Secondly, we have what we may call the desire for reputation or prestige (defining it as respect or esteem from other people), recognition, attention, importance or appreciation.These needs have been relatively stressed by Alfred Adler and his followers, and have been relatively neglected by Freud and the psychoanalysts. More and more today however there is appearing widespread appreciation of their central importance.

Satisfaction of the self-esteem need leads to feelings of self-confidence, worth, strength, capability and adequacy of being useful and necessary in the world. But thwarting of these needs produces feelings of inferiority, of weakness and of helplessness. These feelings in turn give rise to either basic discouragement or else compensatory or neurotic trends. An appreciation of the necessity of basic self-confidence and an understanding of how helpless people are without it can be easily gained from a study of severe traumatic neurosis.

The Need for Self-actualization — Even if all these needs are satisfied, we may still often (if not always) expect that a new discontent and restlessness will soon develop, unless the individual is doing what he is fitted for. A musician must make music, an artist must paint, a poet must write, if he is to be ultimately happy. What a man can be, he must be. This need we may call self-actualization.

This term, first coined by Kurt Goldstein, is being used in this paper in a much more specific and limited fashion. It refers to the desire for self-fulfillment, namely, to the tendency for him to become actualized in what he is potentially. This tendency might be phrased as the desire to become more and more what one is, to become everything that one is capable of becoming.

The specific form that these needs will take will of course vary greatly from person to person. In one individual it may take the form of the desire to be an ideal mother, in another it may be expressed athletically, and in still another it may be expressed in painting pictures or in inventions. It is not necessarily a creative urge although in people who have any capacities for creation it will take this form.

The clear emergence of these needs rests upon prior satisfaction of the physiological, safety, love and esteem needs. We shall call people who are satisfied in these needs, basically satisfied people, and it is from these that we may expect the fullest (and healthiest) creativeness. Since, in our society, basically satisfied people are the exception, we do not know much about self-actualization, either experimentally or clinically. It remains a challenging problem for research.

The preconditions for the basic need satisfactions — There are certain conditions which are immediate prerequisites for the basic need satisfactions. Danger to these is reacted to almost as if it were a direct danger to the basic needs themselves. Such conditions as freedom to speak, freedom to do what one wishes so long as no harm is done to others, freedom to express one's self, freedom to investigate and seek for information, freedom to defend one's self, justice, fairness, honesty, orderliness in the group are examples of such preconditions for basic need satisfactions. Thwarting in these freedoms will be reacted to with a threat or emergency response. These conditions are not ends in themselves but they are almost so since they are so closely related to the basic needs, which are apparently the only ends in themselves. These conditions are defended because without them the basic satisfactions are quite impossible, or at least, very severely endangered.

If we remember that the cognitive capacities (perceptual, intellectual, learning) are a set of adjustive tools, which have, among other functions, that of satisfaction of our basic needs, then it is clear that any danger to them, any deprivation or blocking of their free use, must also be indirectly threatening to the basic needs themselves. Such a statement is a partial solution of the general problems of curiosity, the search for knowledge, truth and wisdom, and the ever-persistent urge to solve the cosmic mysteries.

We must therefore introduce another hypothesis and speak of degrees of closeness to the basic needs, for we have already pointed out that *any* conscious desires (partial goals) are more or less important as they are more or less close to the basic needs. The same statement may be made for various behavior acts. An act is psychologically important if it contributes directly to satisfaction of basic needs. The less directly it so contributes, or the weaker this contribution is, the less important this act must be conceived to be from the point of view of dynamic psychology. A similar statement may be made for the various defense or coping mechanisms. Some are very directly related to the protection or attainment of the basic needs, others are only weakly and distantly related. Indeed if we wished, we could speak of more basic and less basic defense mechanisms, and then affirm that danger to the more basic defenses is more threatening than danger to less basic defenses (always remembering that this is so only because of their relationship to the basic needs).

The desires to know and to understand — So far, we have mentioned the cognitive needs only in passing. Acquiring knowledge and systematizing the universe have been considered as, in part, techniques for the achievement of basic safety in the world, or, for the intelligent man, expressions of self-actualization. Also freedom of inquiry and expression have been discussed as preconditions of satisfactions of the basic needs. True though these formulations may be, they do not constitute definitive answers to the question as to the motivation role of curiosity, learning, philosophizing, experimenting, etc. They are, at best, no more than partial answers.

This question is especially difficult because we know so little about the facts. Curiosity, exploration, desire for the facts, desire to know may certainly be observed easily enough. The fact that they often are pursued even at great cost to the individual's safety is an earnest of the partial character of our previous discussion. In addition, the writer must admit that, though he has sufficient clinical evidence to postulate the desire to know as a very strong drive in intelligent people, no data are available for unintelligent people. It may then be largely a function of relatively high intelligence. Rather tentatively, then, and largely in the hope of stimulating discussion and research, we shall postulate a basic desire to know, to be aware of reality, to get the facts, to satisfy curiosity, or as Wertheimer phrases it, to see rather than to be blind.

This postulation, however, is not enough. Even after we know, we are impelled to know more and more minutely and microscopically on the one hand, and on the other, more and more extensively in the direction of a world philosophy, religion, etc. The facts that we acquire, if they are isolated or atomistic, inevitably get theorized about, and either analyzed or organized or both. This process has been phrased by some as the search for 'meaning.' We shall then postulate a desire to understand, to systematize, to organize, to analyze, to look for relations and meanings.

Once these desires are accepted for discussion, we see that they too form themselves into a small hierarchy in which the desire to know is prepotent over the desire to understand. All the characteristics of a hierarchy of prepotency that we have described above, seem to hold for this one as well.

We must guard ourselves against the too easy tendency to separate these desires from the basic needs we have discussed above, *i.e.*, to make a sharp dichotomy between 'cognitive' and 'conative' needs. The desire to know and to understand are themselves conative, i.e., have a striving character, and are as much personality needs as the 'basic needs' we have already discussed.

Further Characteristics of the Basic Needs

The degree of fixity of the hierarchy of basic needs. — We have spoken so far as if this hierarchy were a fixed order but actually it is not nearly as rigid as we may have implied. It is true that most of the people with whom we have worked have seemed to have these basic needs in about the order that has been indicated. However, there have been a number of exceptions.

(1) There are some people in whom, for instance, self-esteem seems to be more important than love. This most common reversal in the hierarchy is usually due to the development of the notion that the person who is most likely to be loved is a strong or powerful person, one who inspires respect or fear, and who is self confident or aggressive. Therefore such people who lack love and seek it, may try hard to put on a front of aggressive, confident behavior. But essentially they seek high self-esteem and its behavior expressions more as a means-to-an-end than for its own sake; they seek self-assertion for the sake of love rather than for self-esteem itself.

(2) There are other, apparently innately creative people in whom the drive to creativeness seems to be more important than any other counter-determinant. Their creativeness might appear not as self-actualization released by basic satisfaction, but in spite of lack of basic satisfaction.

(3) In certain people the level of aspiration may be permanently deadened or lowered. That is to say, the less pre-potent goals may simply be lost, and may disappear forever, so that the person who has experienced life at a very low level, *i. e.,* chronic unemployment, may continue to be satisfied for the rest of his life if only he can get enough food.

(4) The so-called 'psychopathic personality' is another example of permanent loss of the love needs. These are people who, according to the best data available,

have been starved for love in the earliest months of their lives and have simply lost forever the desire and the ability to give and to receive affection (as animals lose sucking or pecking reflexes that are not exercised soon enough after birth).

(5) Another cause of reversal of the hierarchy is that when a need has been satisfied for a long time, this need may be underevaluated. People who have never experienced chronic hunger are apt to underestimate its effects and to look upon food as a rather unimportant thing. If they are dominated by a higher need, this higher need will seem to be the most important of all. It then becomes possible, and indeed does actually happen, that they may, for the sake of this higher need, put themselves into the position of being deprived in a more basic need. We may expect that after a long-time deprivation of the more basic need there will be a tendency to reevaluate both needs so that the more pre-potent need will actually become consciously prepotent for the individual who may have given it up very lightly. Thus, a man who has given up his job rather than lose his self-respect, and who then starves for six months or so, may be willing to take his job back even at the price of losing his a self-respect.

(6) Another partial explanation of *apparent* reversals is seen in the fact that we have been talking about the hierarchy of prepotency in terms of consciously felt wants or desires rather than of behavior. Looking at behavior itself may give us the wrong impression. What we have claimed is that the person will want the more basic of two needs when deprived in both. There is no necessary implication here that he will act upon his desires. Let us say again that there are many determinants of behavior other than the needs and desires.

(7) Perhaps more important than all these exceptions are the ones that involve ideals, high social

> standards, high values and the like. With such values people become martyrs; they give up everything for the sake of a particular ideal, or value. These people may be understood, at least in part, by reference to one basic concept (or hypothesis) which may be called 'increased frustration-tolerance through early gratification'. People who have been satisfied in their basic needs throughout their lives, particularly in their earlier years, seem to develop exceptional power to withstand present or future thwarting of these needs simply because they have strong,[p. 388] healthy character structure as a result of basic satisfaction. They are the 'strong' people who can easily weather disagreement or opposition, who can swim against the stream of public opinion and who can stand up for the truth at great personal cost. It is just the ones who have loved and been well loved, and who have had many deep friendships who can hold out against hatred, rejection or persecution.

For instance, it is likely that those persons who have been accustomed to relative starvation for a long time, are partially enabled thereby to withstand food deprivation. What sort of balance must be made between these two tendencies, of habituation on the one hand, and of past satisfaction breeding present frustration tolerance on the other hand, remains to be worked out by further research. Meanwhile we may assume that they are both operative, side by side, since they do not contradict each other, in respect to this phenomenon of increased frustration tolerance, it seems probable that the most important gratifications come in the first two years of life. That is to say, people who have been made secure and strong in the earliest years, tend to remain secure and strong thereafter in the face of whatever threatens.

Degree of relative satisfaction – So far, our theoretical discussion may have given the impression that these five sets of needs are somehow in a step-wise, all-or-none relationships to each other. We have spoken in such terms as the following:

"If one need is satisfied, then another emerges." This statement might give the false impression that a need must be satisfied 100 per cent before the next need emerges. In actual fact, most members of our society who are normal, are partially satisfied in all their basic needs and partially unsatisfied in all their basic needs at the same time. A more realistic description of the hierarchy would be in terms of decreasing percentages of satisfaction as we go up the hierarchy of prepotency, For instance, if I may assign arbitrary figures for the sake of illustration, it is as if the average citizen is satisfied perhaps 85 per cent in his physiological needs, 70 per cent in his safety needs, 50 per cent in his love needs, 40 per cent in his self-esteem needs, and 10 per cent in his self-actualization needs.

As for the concept of emergence of a new need after satisfaction of the prepotent need, this emergence is not a sudden, saltatory phenomenon but rather a gradual emergence by slow degrees from nothingness. For instance, if prepotent need A is satisfied only 10 per cent: then need B may not be visible at all. However, as this need A becomes satisfied 25 per cent, need B may emerge 5 per cent, as need A becomes satisfied 75 per cent need B may emerge go per cent, and so on.

Unconscious character of needs — These needs are neither necessarily conscious nor unconscious. On the whole, however, in the average person, they are more often unconscious rather than conscious. It is not necessary at this point to overhaul the tremendous mass of evidence which indicates the crucial importance of unconscious motivation. It would by now be expected, on a priori grounds alone, that unconscious motivations would on the whole be rather more important than the conscious motivations. What we have called the basic needs are very often largely unconscious although they may, with suitable techniques, and with sophisticated people become conscious.

Cultural specificity and generality of needs — This classification of basic needs makes some attempt to take account of the relative unity behind the superficial differences in specific desires from one culture to another. Certainly in any particular culture an individual's conscious motivational content will usually be extremely different from the conscious motivational content of an individual in another society. However, it is the common experience of anthropologists that people, even in different societies, are much more alike than we would think from our first contact with them, and that as we know them better we seem to find more and more of this commonness, We then recognize the most startling differences to be superficial rather than basic, *e. g.*, differences in style of hair-dress, clothes, tastes in food, etc. Our classification of basic needs is in part an attempt to account for this unity behind the apparent diversity from culture to culture. No claim is made that it is ultimate or universal for all cultures. The claim is made only that it is relatively more ultimate, more universal, more basic, than the superficial conscious desires from culture to culture, and makes a somewhat closer approach to common-human characteristics, Basic needs are more common-human than superficial desires or behaviors.

Multiple motivations of behavior — These needs must be understood not to be exclusive or single determiners of certain kinds of behavior. An example may be found in any behavior that seems to be physiologically motivated, such as eating, or sexual play or the like. The clinical psychologists have long since found that any behavior may be a channel through which flow various determinants. Or to say it in another way, most behavior is multi-motivated. Within the sphere of motivational determinants any behavior tends to be determined by several or all of the basic needs simultaneously rather than by only one of them. The latter would be more an exception than the former. Eating may be partially for the sake of filling the stomach, and partially for the sake of comfort and amelioration of other needs.

One may make love not only for pure sexual release, but also to convince one's self of one's masculinity, or to make a conquest, to feel powerful, or to win more basic affection. As an illustration, I may point out that it would be possible (theoretically if not practically) to analyze a single act of an individual and see in it the expression of his physiological needs, his safety needs, his love needs, his esteem needs and self-actualization. This contrasts sharply with the more naive brand of trait psychology in which one trait or one motive accounts for a certain kind of act, i. e., an aggressive act is traced solely to a trait of aggressiveness.

Multiple determinants of behavior – Not all behavior is determined by the basic needs. We might even say that not all behavior is motivated. There are many determinants of behavior other than motives. For instance, one other important class of determinants is the so-called 'field' determinants. Theoretically, at least, behavior may be determined completely by the field, or even by specific isolated external stimuli, as in association of ideas, or certain conditioned reflexes. If in response to the stimulus word 'table' I immediately perceive a memory image of a table, this response certainly has nothing to do with my basic needs.

Secondly, we may call attention again to the concept of 'degree of closeness to the basic needs' or 'degree of motivation.' Some behavior is highly motivated; other behavior is only weakly motivated. Some is not motivated at all (but all behavior is determined).

Another important point is that there is a basic difference between expressive behavior and coping behavior (functional striving, purposive goal seeking). An expressive behavior does not try to do anything; it is simply a reflection of the personality. A stupid man behaves stupidly, not because he wants to, or tries to, or is motivated to, but simply because he is what he is. The same is true when I speak in a bass voice rather than tenor or soprano. The random movements of a healthy child, the smile on the face of a happy man even when he is alone, the springiness of the healthy man's walk, and the erectness of his carriage are other examples of expressive, non-functional behavior. Also the style in which a man carries out almost all his behavior, motivated as well as unmotivated, is often expressive.

We may then ask, is *all* behavior expressive or reflective of the character structure? The answer is 'No.' Rote, habitual, automatized, or conventional behavior may or may not be expressive. The same is true for most 'stimulus-bound' behaviors. It is finally necessary to stress that expressiveness of behavior, and goal-directedness of behavior are not mutually exclusive categories. Average behavior is usually both.

Goals as centering principle in motivation theory — It will be observed that the basic principle in our classification has been neither the instigation nor the motivated behavior but rather the functions, effects, purposes, or goals of the behavior. It has been proven sufficiently by various people that this is the most suitable point for centering in any motivation theory.

Animal- and human-centering — This theory starts with the human being rather than any lower and presumably 'simpler' animal. Too many of the findings that have been made in animals have been proven to be true for animals but not for the human being. There is no reason whatsoever why we should start with animals in order to study human motivation. The logic or rather illogic behind this general fallacy of 'pseudo-simplicity' has been exposed often enough by philosophers and logicians as well as by scientists in each of the various fields. It is no more necessary to study animals before one can study man than it is to study mathematics before one can study geology or psychology or biology.

We may also reject the old, naive, behaviorism which assumed that it was somehow necessary, or at least more 'scientific' to judge human beings by animal standards. One consequence of this belief was that the whole notion of purpose and goal was excluded from motivational psychology simply because one could not ask a white rat about his purposes. Tolman has long since proven in animal studies themselves that this exclusion was not necessary.

Motivation and the theory of psychopathogenesis — The conscious motivational content of everyday life has, according to the foregoing, been conceived to be relatively important or unimportant accordingly as it is more or less closely related to the basic goals. A desire for an ice cream cone might actually be an indirect expression of a desire for love. If it is, then this desire for the ice cream cone becomes extremely important motivation. If however the ice cream is simply something to cool the mouth with, or a casual appetitive reaction, then the desire is relatively unimportant. Everyday conscious desires are to be regarded as symptoms, surface *indicators of more basic needs*. If we were to take these superficial desires at their face value we would find ourselves in a state of complete confusion which could never be resolved, since we would be dealing seriously with symptoms rather than with what lay behind the symptoms.

Thwarting of unimportant desires produces no psychopathological results; thwarting of a basically important need does produce such results. Any theory of psychopathogenesis must then be based on a sound theory of motivation. A conflict or a frustration is not necessarily pathogenic. It becomes so only when it threatens or thwarts the basic needs, or partial needs that are closely related to the basic needs.

The role of gratified needs – It has been pointed out above several times that our needs usually emerge only when more prepotent needs have been gratified. Thus gratification has an important role in motivation theory. Apart from this, however, needs cease to play an active determining or organizing role as soon as they are gratified.

What this means is that, *e. g.*, a basically satisfied person no longer has the needs for esteem, love, safety, etc. The only sense in which he might be said to have them is in the almost metaphysical sense that a sated man has hunger, or a filled bottle has emptiness. If we are interested in what *actually* motivates us, and not in what has, will, or might motivate us, then a satisfied need is not a motivator. It must be considered for all practical purposes simply not to exist, to have disappeared. This point should be emphasized because it has been either overlooked or contradicted in every theory of motivation. The perfectly healthy, normal, fortunate man has no sex needs or hunger needs, or needs for safety, or for love, or for prestige, or self-esteem, except in stray moments of quickly passing threat. If we were to say otherwise, we should also have to aver that every man had all the pathological reflexes, *e. g.*, Babinski, etc., because if his nervous system were damaged, these would appear.

It is such considerations as these that suggest the bold postulation that a man who is thwarted in any of his basic needs may fairly be envisaged simply as a sick man. This is a fair parallel to our designation as 'sick' of the man who lacks vitamins or minerals. Who is to say that a lack of love is less important than a lack of vitamins? Since we know the pathogenic effects of love starvation, who is to say that we are invoking value-questions in an unscientific or illegitimate way, any more than the physician does who diagnoses and treats pellagra or scurvy? If a man has any other basic needs in any active, chronic sense, then he is simply an unhealthy man. He is as surely sick as if he had suddenly developed a strong salt-hunger or calcium hunger.

If this statement seems unusual or paradoxical the reader may be assured that this is only one among many such paradoxes that will appear as we revise our ways of looking at man's deeper motivations. When we ask what man wants of life, we deal with his very essence.

(1) There are at least five sets of goals, which we may call basic needs. These are briefly physiological, safety, love, 'esteem, and self-actualization. In addition, we are motivated by the desire to achieve or maintain the various conditions upon which these basic satisfactions rest and by certain more intellectual desires.

(2) These basic goals are related to each other, being arranged in a hierarchy of prepotency. This means that the most prepotent goal will monopolize consciousness and will tend of itself to organize the

recruitment of the various capacities of the organism. The less prepotent needs are minimized, even forgotten or denied. But when a need is fairly well satisfied, the next prepotent ('higher') need emerges, in turn to dominate the conscious life and to serve as the center of organization of behavior, since gratified needs are not active motivators.

Thus man is a perpetually wanting animal. Ordinarily the satisfaction of these wants is not altogether mutually exclusive, but only tends to be. The average member of our society is most often partially satisfied and partially unsatisfied in all of his wants. The hierarchy principle is usually empirically observed in terms of increasing percentages of non-satisfaction as we go up the hierarchy. Reversals of the average order of the hierarchy are sometimes observed. Also it has been observed that an individual may permanently lose the higher wants in the hierarchy under special conditions. There are not only ordinarily multiple motivations for usual behavior, but in addition many determinants other than motives.

(3) Any thwarting or possibility of thwarting of these basic human goals, or danger to the defenses which protect them, or to the conditions upon which they rest, is considered to be a psychological threat. With a few exceptions, all psychopathology may be partially traced to such threats. A basically thwarted man may actually be defined as a 'sick' man, if we wish.

(4) It is such basic threats which bring about the general emergency reactions.

(5) Certain other basic problems have not been dealt with because of limitations of space. Among these are (a) the problem of values in any definitive motivation theory, (b) the relation between appetites, desires, needs and what is 'good' for the

organism, (*c*) the etiology of the basic needs and their possible derivation in early childhood, (*d*) redefinition of motivational concepts, *i. e.*, drive, desire, wish, need, goal, (*e*) implication of our theory for hedonistic theory, (*f*) the nature of the uncompleted act, of success and failure, and of aspiration-level, (*g*) the role of association, habit and conditioning, (*h*) relation to the theory of interpersonal relations, (*i*) implications for psychotherapy, (*j*) implication for theory of society, (k) the theory of selfishness, (*l*) the relation between needs and cultural patterns, (*m*) the relation between this theory and Alport's theory of functional autonomy. These as well as certain other less important questions must be considered as motivation theory attempts to become definitive.

Chapter 4

Employment Conditions for Marine

General Conditions

Successful candidates must obtain and maintain an appropriate security clearance.

Successful candidates may require mandatory qualifications and will have to obtain an AMSA medical certificate.

Qualifications and Training

Applicants will require the following minimum mandatory qualifications prior to applying for the following positions:

- Master Class 4 (Level 3 Commanding Officers)
- Engineer Class 3 (Level 3 Engineers)
- Master Class 5 - endorsed to 200nm and MED Grade 2 (Level 2 Watch keepers)

During probation, all officers will be required to successfully complete:

- Marine Induction Training Course
- Use of Force Training
- Bay-class Familiarisation / Work Up Training
- Deck-mounted machine gun training (MAG58) and will be required to obtain:
- A St John Ambulance Association Red Cross Society Senior First Aid Certificate and

- An Occupational Health and Safety at Sea or Elements of Shipboard Safety Course.
- AMSA medical certificate

Officers will be required to maintain mandatory qualifications and certificates/permits while employed with the National Marine Unit.

Probationary Period

Successful applicants are subject to a 12-month probationary period generally consisting of a full-time training component and on-the-job assessment during which time satisfactory work performance and conduct consistent with the APS Code of Conduct is required. Progress is carefully monitored during probation and Customs may terminate employment at any time in the probation period. Termination of employment is usually only considered when progress is assessed as unsatisfactory, for examples, as indicated by performance and attendance.

Salary and Allowances

Salary and allowances are covered by the Customs Certified Agreement 2004-2007. To offset the demands placed on marine officers to ensure maximum flexibility in utilisation, deployment and crewing of Customs seagoing vessels, a Commuted Marine Allowance applies upon assignment to seagoing duties onboard an ACV. See the Certified Agreement (Section 9. Marine Conditions) for further details.

Domiciling

See the Certified Agreement (Section 7. Domestic Travel and Assignment to Another Locality) and the NMU Domiciling Policy.

Selection Process

- The selection process will be merit based and may include:
- Screening of applications
- Aptitude and psychometric testing

- Panel interview
- Security check
- Reference/referee checks
- Medical examination

Applicants will only be considered for these steps if they initially meet the selection criteria.

Security Clearance

Customs Officers hold a position of trust and must deal properly with sensitive information at times. As a result, all positions in Customs are security assessed positions and candidates must pass a security clearance before being made an offer of a position.

The security assessment is conducted by Customs in compliance with the Commonwealth Protective Security Manual.

The security assessment includes background checks and you will be required to provide detailed personal information. This may include details of your employment and residence history, financial circumstances, any criminal charges and/or convictions (including traffic offences), any drug use and any overseas travel. You may also be required to provide this kind of information about your spouse, partner or defacto where applicable.

You will also be asked to provide contact details for at least three referees who will be contacted by Customs directly. Your referees will be asked to answer probing questions about your suitability for employment as a Customs Officer.

Medical Examination

All National Marine Unit officers are required to obtain an AMSA Certificate of Medical Fitness for Deck/Catering/ Engine. Officers are required to be in an adequate state of health and physical fitness to competently perform the required duties. The medical examination will assess your general health and mobility as well as your eyesight and hearing.

AMSA Oral Exam, Cert Compt, Master and Chief Mate (Unlimited), Master and Chief Mate

Notes to Candidates

1. It should be noted that the following is not a fully detailed list of orals questions, but a list of topics about which candidates are expected to have adequate knowledge, and is provided for the guidance of candidates only.
2. The Examiner may ask any questions relevant to the following topic areas, and / or ask the candidate to provide answers in diagrammatic form, or to complete simple calculations, to the extent necessary to test the candidate's competency in the managerial, operational and safety aspects related to the duties of the grade of certificate applied for.
3. Candidates for both Masters and Chief Mates grade of certificate can be asked questions from all sections listed, however the focus of the questions and the assessment, will be related to the main management responsibilities and shipboard duties involved in the certificate being applied for.
4. As this syllabus also incorporates the syllabus for lower grade certificates, the Examiner may ask questions related to those lower grade certificates as it effects the overall safe operation of the vessel.
5. Candidates should note that they may be required to demonstrate their proficiency in RADAR plotting and chart-work.
6. During the examination, candidates will be required to demonstrate that they possess an adequate knowledge and understanding in the use of the English language.

Management of Regulatory and Ship's Administration

- Knowledge of ship inspection and survey programmes and the roll of Port State control and Flag State Control Officers.

- Knowledge of a ships certification, documentation and records.
- Knowledge of classification societies, classification and surveys of ships and equipment.
- Knowledge of appropriate Australian legislation, statutory requirements, including the ISM Code and the application thereof.
- Knowledge of relevant International Codes and Conventions and the application thereof.
- Knowledge of Australian OH and S legislation as it applies to the maritime industry.
- Ship administration duties, shipmasters business and carriage of goods by sea.
- Joining a vessel and the responsibilities and duties of shipboard personnel.

STCW Standards of Watch-keeping

- Principals to be observed in keeping a watch in port, on the bridge watch at sea, at anchor and under pilotage.
- Voyage planning berth to berth
- Bridge resource management

Bridge Equipment

Knowledge of the different types of bridge and navigation equipment, along with the operation, testing, errors and precautions associated with the use of such equipment.

Navigation, Charts and Publications

- Maintenance and practical knowledge of nautical publications and charts.
- Knowledge of ship reporting systems and the promulgation of all relevant maritime safety information.
- Knowledge of the use of charts and interpretation of charted information, including the general principles of voyage planning.

- Knowledge of all aspects of practical navigation and obtaining tidal information required by senior management shipboard personnel.

Stress and Stability

- Practical knowledge and use of all relevant sources of information to safely load a vessel and assess a vessel's stability condition, trim and list.
- Principles of ship stability
- Knowledge of Load lines and seasonal zones, drafts and the effects of changes in water density
- Knowledge of the different types of shipboard stresses and means of reducing such stresses.
- Management of free surface effects

Cargo Work

- Knowledge of Australian and international legislation, and detailed knowledge of the requirements, relating to the carriage, stowage, securing, loading and unloading of cargoes on various types of vessels.
- Knowledge of typical cargo handling equipment found on various types of vessels.
- Knowledge of all aspects on confined space entry
- Knowledge of the carriage of dangerous goods

Ship Handling

- Knowledge of manoeuvring techniques, principles and characteristics for the main ship types, and their propulsion systems.
- Knowledge of the safe principles of mooring and unmooring, anchoring and heaving to
- Knowledge of the use of tugs and anchors
- Knowledge of interaction and other factors affecting manoeuvring in narrow channels and shallow water
- Knowledge of the principles for the safe embarking and disembarking of a pilot, and launch and recovery of rescue craft

- Management of vessel in adverse weather and the effect of wave impact on a vessel, the effect of adverse weather on various ship operations involving manoeuvring

Prevention of Pollution

- Knowledge of Australian and International legislation in relation to pollution
- Safe management principles of all relevant shipboard precautions to prevent pollution.
- Knowledge of the actions to be taken in event of a pollution incident
- Knowledge of bunkering precautions

Emergency Situations / Response and Equipment

- Knowledge of contemporary safety issues, reports and papers, affecting the maritime industry
- Management level response to various shipboard emergency situations both in port and at sea
- Principles of damage control and salvage
- Obligations to render assistance and in sending emergency signals
- Knowledge of the safe management of helicopter operations
- Knowledge of the safe principles of towing operations

Dry Docking

- Preparations for docking and undocking including stability issues
- Precautions and dangers whilst in dock
- Management of OH and S issues in dock

Search and Rescue

- Knowledge of search and rescue publications, procedures, communications and equipment
- Knowledge of survival techniques

Essential Shipboard Equipment and Machinery

- Knowledge of the operation of various types of shipboard fire fighting and life saving equipment, together with an understanding of the associated safety aspects and precautions related to operation of such equipment.
- Operation, maintenance and inspection requirements of essential shipboard equipment and machinery
- Management and organisation of statutory drills.
- Knowledge of all factors affecting the watertight integrity of the ship
- Knowledge of correct operation of on load release gear for survival craft

Collision Avoidance and Buoyage

- The application and content of the International Regulations for Preventing Collisions at Sea Collision avoidance
- Knowledge of the internationally adopted system of buoyage.

STANDARDS REGARDING THE ENGINE DEPARTMENT

Mandatory minimum requirements for certification of officers in charge of an engineering watch in a manned engine-room or designated duty engineers in a periodically unmanned engine-room.

Training

The education and training required by paragraph 2.3 of regulation III/1 shall include training in mechanical and electrical workshop skills relevant to the duties of an engineer officer.

On-board Training

Every candidate for certification as officer in charge of an engineering watch in a manned engine-room or as designated duty engineer in a periodically unmanned engine-room of ships powered by main propulsion machinery of 750 kW or more shall follow an approved programme of on-board training which:

i. Ensures that during the required period of seagoing service the candidate receives systematic practical training and experience in the tasks, duties and responsibilities of an officer in charge of an engine-room watch, taking into account the guidance given in section B-III/1 of this Code;

ii. Is closely supervised and monitored by a qualified and certificated engineer officer aboard the ships in which the approved seagoing service is performed; and

iii. Is adequately documented in a training record book.

Contract of Employment

Contract of As soon as you take on an employee to work for you, you should draw up a contract of employment which sets out the relationship between you and your employee. The contract should be based on issues and tasks you felt should be legally binding between you and your employee, and can both agree upon; an example might be the paid holidays the employee is entitled to.

It is always best to draw up a contract of employment rather than to do this verbally, as this will prevent any disputes arising from what was said or not said when the employee was taken on. Also, written contracts should be worded clearly to avoid ambiguity or misinterpretation. The document should be signed and dated by both parties; this contract should be given to the employee, but a copy kept on file for your own reference.

The Content

What you include in your contract of employment will depend on what job you are offering and under what terms, but you must also include "written particulars" as part of your contract to comply with The Employment Rights Act 1996.

You should also be very careful when outlining an employees job description if you would like your employee to show flexibility in their job role. If you are too rigid with the tasks outlined you will prevent flexibility. To prevent disputes as a result of wording or being too vague it is best to draw a balance between being too rigid and formal and too flexible and informal as tipping the balance either way could cause a dispute. The rule is to think carefully before you define a job description.

Written Particulars

Written particulars have to be included to break down or explain in detail about the terms and conditions of employment, and by law you are required to provide these details to your employee. You may decide to provide a brief outline of your terms and conditions of employment within one document, and then provide a secondary document which outlines the contract in more details; however, your employees have the write to written particulars no later than two month's after beginning employment with you.

It is important that you are familiar with the particulars which you are required to be included within any contract of employment, and therefore it advised that you obtain and study the Employment rights Act 1996.

The following are particulars which must be provided to your employee:

- The parties of the contract i.e. your company's name and address and your employees name and address
- The date the contract began
- The scale or rate of pay or the method of calculating pay
- How intervals the employee will get paid weekly, monthly or any other specific interval
- Terms and conditions relating to the hours of work - normal hours, overtime, expected out of hours work
- The job title

- A brief description of what the employee is expect to do
- Where the employee will be working giving the address(es) or locations
- Terms relating to injury and sickness and sick-pay
- Provisions for sick pay
- Pension schemes or pension policy
- Terms and conditions to holiday entitlement
- A brief disciplinary summary (a code of conduct and disciplinary manual should be provided on request)
- If the job is part-time, temporary or contractual
- If contractual contract you need to state when the contract ends
- The length of notice to terminate their contract
- Any collective agreements which might affect the terms and conditions
- If the employee is required to work outside the UK you must include the period he or she is to work outside the UK, the currency in which you will pay the employee, any benefits which you may have provided for your employee to work outside the UK and any terms and conditions relating to the employees return to the UK

Chapter 5

Motivating Employees

MOTIVATING YOUR CREW

A complaint arises everywhere that they can't find hardworking employees. In reality, it's our management style that determines the efforts of our workers. Here are a few tips that work to motivate the crew.

Have the right attitude. If you display a negative or casual attitude toward your work, so will the people who work for you. Even though you may still work hard, others will slack because of it.

Although the master and crew are responsible for ensuring the vessel is maintained in a safe and efficient condition, the manager is responsible for maintaining the vessel in line with requirements of the owner and agreed level of safety by company standard. This includes having a properly motivated crew and ensuring they have the necessary tools and materials required to carry out the required maintenance. The ship manager is contractually responsible for maintenance however the owner is ultimately responsible for the condition of the vessels as he is the one who sets the budget!

In today's current market environment we are being driven more and more towards zero defect acceptability by new regulation and the application of these regulations by Port State Control, Coast Guard and other bodies. Therefore we must endeavour to employ best practice in maintenance and management methods to achieve a safe yet cost effective solution.

Best practice starts at the new building contract stage where every effort and some extra cash should be invested in putting together a vessel that will not only operate efficiently but will have low through life maintenance costs.

The budget is the basic tool to set the expenditure required to maintain the vessels and against which the superintendent will measure and control this expenditure.

Good 'housekeeping' is imperative such as keeping machinery clean and areas tidy.

Both housekeeping instruction, basic watch keeping and good direction are essential as is good housekeeping and accurate recording of conditions monitored. Conditions monitored is the testing of alarms and control which are critical as personnel safety and the safety of the ship depends on it.

Best practice as a review of maintenance and records and keeping a continuous look out on all aspects of the vessel - whether scheduling a program or not.

Best practice is using the correct materials and skill sets to carry out maintenance tasks. The hull and structure and tanks need to be dealt with in the same way therefore regular inspections and assessments leading to remedial action when required.

Set a realistic budget that will allow you to carry out the required maintenance. Keep things clean and ensure the crews are trained in the menial tasks. Set the optimum level of maintenance. Monitor conditions diligently and initiate corrective action when necessary. Utilise a suitable planned maintenance system that can be understood and used by the crew without extensive training. Present trends are towards computer software packages and these can be powerful tools when used properly.

Record work done clearly and accurately. Work closely with classification societies.

Have properly trained crew on board.

Keep the crew motivated with a reasonable wage level, job security and a sense of belonging. Make sure the crew have job satisfaction and know what is required of them and that they will be given the tools and materials to do the job. Give the crew proper training to perform competently and safely and give them feedback on how they are performing.

Untrained, inexperienced and insufficiently skilled operating engineers will ensure disaster no matter how good the ship and its machinery is. Training is vital for sea and shore staff. V.Ships use extensive shore based and onboard training programs to enhance the quality and productivity of their crews.

The manager is required to operate the vessel in a safe and efficient manner in compliance with all the class, national and international rules and regulations that apply.

The manger must provide a competent, professionally capable and cost effective crew who are in possession of all the necessary certification for the particular size and type of vessel.

The manager must set up and operate a workable and effective planned maintenance system to maintain the vessel within the limits of the Manager and Owner expectations and as required under the ISM Code, but always to operate within safe parameters and minimise risk.

THE MARINE CREW

Marine Engineers are the officers of a ship that operate and maintain the propulsion and other systems onboard the vessel. Marine Engineering staff also deal with the "Hotel" facilities onboard, notably the sewage, lighting, air conditioning and water systems. They deal with bulk fuel transfers, and require training in firefighting and first aid, as well as in dealing with the ship's boats and other nautical tasks-especially with cargo loading/discharging gear and safety systems, though the specific cargo discharge function remains the responsibility of deck officers and deck workers.

Sometimes, they are involved in the design and construction of these complicated systems. New design is mostly included within the naval architecture or ship design. The field is closely related to mechanical engineering, although the modern engineer requires knowledge (and hands on experience) with electrical, electronic, pneumatic, hydraulic, chemistry, control engineering, naval architecture, process engineering, gas turbines and even nuclear technology on certain military vessels.

A ship's crew is divided into two distinct sections: those who navigate the ship and those who maintain it. The navigators are deck officers and report to the Master (also functionally referred to as Captain), and engineers whose charge is the running and maintenance of all machinery report to the Chief engineer. Also on board are 'ratings' who are experienced hands who, though not officers, play a key role in assisting the officers in daily operations. In the Engine department, this includes electricians, motormen (or fitters, depending on nomanclature), oilers, wipers, and utilitymen who play a large role in the daily upkeep of the engine room.

The original term engineer on a ship meant the people who dealt with the engines ("The black hand gang"), as opposed to the Consulting Engineer concept. Marine Engineers are generally much more hands on, and often get dirty, sweaty and work in arduous conditions with temperatures in the engine room spaces exceeding 50 degrees Celsius (122 degrees Fahrenheit). Care and a clear head need to be maintained at all times, however, especially with heavy machinery in a seaway, and in managing the rest of the engine-room crew.

There are 4 classifications of Marine Engineering licences throughout the merchant marine, those being Chief Engineer, First Assistant/Second Engineer, Second Assistant/Third Engineer, and Third Assistant/Fourth Engineer.

Personnel

A common Engineering crew for a ship is:

- (1) Chief Engineer
- (1) Second Engineer / First Assistant Engineer

- (1) Third Engineer / Second Assistant Engineer
- (1-2) Fourth Engineer / Third Assistant Engineer
- (0-2) Fifth Engineer / Junior Engineer
- (1-3) Oiler (unlicenced qualified rating)
- (0-3) Greaser/s (unlicensed qualified rating)
- (1-5) Entry-level rating (such as Wiper, Utilityman, etc)

Insignia

Engineer Officers bear the same number of stripes on epaulettes as Deck Officers with complementary rank. For instance, a Chief Engineer bears 4 stripes, as a Captain does, but they are distinguished by the epaulettes bearing the Engineer's Blue. There is a popular legend that Engineers wear the color in honor of the RMS Titanic's Engineers who never abandoned their stations and went down with the ship. But that colorful story is not quite the source of the honour. In the 1830s, Joseph Whitworth invented the method of making truly accurate flat surfaces by using Engineer's blue. The method is also used for testing bearing and journal surfaces. It is this color that Engineers wear.

A different means of differentiating engineering officers from deck officers is by the device above the stripes. In some merchant fleets, a propeller device is located above the engineer's stripes while an anchor is located above the deck officer's stripes.

How To Get Crew Qualified

The Coast Guard Auxiliary has a number of privately owned vessels that have been offered for use by their owners. These private vessels are inspected annually and are equipped by their owners with specific safety and rescue equipment on board. There is almost always a need for more operational vessels in all the operating areas of the Auxiliary in Alaska. The Auxiliary also has the operational responsibility for three SAFE Boats that were owned and maintained by the Coast Guard for use primarily in South Central Alaska waters by the Auxiliary. All these vessels need specially trained crews to operate them. The minimum staffing requirements for these boats is one coxswain and one crew member. To operate the "SAFE Boats" the coxswain and crew member must be specifically qualified as UTM qualified.

Boats having the required minimum crew can obtain orders to patrol in their area of responsibility. The appropriate Coast Guard unit will establish a communications schedule and the boat will report their location and status on a regular basis. Crew members will be required to wear prescribed personal protective gear. Operational vessels on orders may be reimbursed for the fuel used during their patrols.

Training

To become a crew member one needs to be motivated and fairly patient. The process does not occur overnight and there are a number of expenses related to the task. Crew members, and also coxswains, must dedicate a considerable amount of time to learning the necessary material. A number of books must be obtained and studied. Several Operational Specialty Courses are offered periodically and are highly recommended for crew members. While not specifically required, crew members often maintain current certification in First Aid and/ or CPR.

The bulk of the training is demonstrated by checking off specific tasks. Crew members have specific check offs they must accomplish and coxswains have their own list of skills to demonstrate. When the prospective crew member has studied and learned a particular skill, their proficiency is demonstrated before a mentor. Mentors are members who are already crew or coxswain qualified who are specifically identified by a flotilla commander as a mentor. An existing crew member can mentor prospective crew members and an existing coxswain can mentor both prospective crew and coxswains. Members with special professional training (such as a medical professional) may also act a mentor for their expertise, even if not qualified in the Boat Crew Program. When all the required tasks have been successfully demonstrated before a mentor, a final test of the prospective crew member/coxswain is made by a Qualifying Examiner or QE. The QE will perform a comprehensive dock side exam covering the topics previously covered with the mentor and will seek successful demonstration of proficiency of the required tasks during a check ride aboard an operational vessel. The QE can chose from any of the topics covered with a mentor for the dockside exam. It is therefore important to be well prepared before going before the QE.

Training for a crew member frequently begins with land based training and check off sessions. In these sessions, learning and the actual application of the skills is demonstrated before a mentor(s). Trainees learn marlinspike, navigation, and the use of fire extinguishers, among other topics. Successfully completing the land based skills early in the year will result in less "classroom" or off the water time when summer finally arrives. Most of the remaining skills are those that can only be learned and demonstrated on the water. Platforms for the water based training may include being a trainee aboard a "SAFE Boat". A maximum of two trainees may be scheduled on any given mission aboard a "SAFE Boats". Sign up with the operational officer or Auxiliary Leader In Charge (LINC) to receive this wonderful on the water training. Search and rescue exercises (SAREXes) are scheduled at many ports/ harbors throughout the summer and are also great opportunities to learn on the on-water skills. Even members without a boat and with some advanced planning, can come out for the training during the day or an entire weekend on an operational facility.

The boat crew qualification guide contains the actual skills a crew member needs to demonstrate before a mentor and ultimately a QE. Prospective crew members are allowed two years to demonstrate skills, have mentors sign this book and appear before a Coxswain for the oral exam and check ride. Bring this guide to the team coordination training session that is required of all crew members and have the guide when on land and water training sessions. This guide contains a study guide in the back to lead the prospective crew member to areas to become familiar with. It also has the check-off items and skills you will need to answer and master. The guide also contains a sign-off sheet that is turned into the Director of Auxiliary in Juneau by the QE when completed for review and certification as a crewman.

The third manual is the boat crew seamanship manual. This reference book covers everything from anchors to weighing anchors and is used by both prospective crew members and coxswains.

Chapter 6

Staff Organisation

A staff helps an expert get all his work done. To this end, a "chief of staff" decides whether an assignment is routine or not. If it's routine, he assigns it to a staff member, who is a sort of junior expert. The chief of staff schedules the routine problems, and checks that they are completed.

If a problem is not routine, the chief of staff notices. He passes it to the expert, who solves the problem, and educates the staff – converting the problem into a routine problem.

In a "cross functional team", like an executive committee, the boss *has* to be a non-expert, because so many kinds of expertise are required.

Basics and General Guidelines

- What are the primary goals and objectives that the organization should be designed to meet?
- What continuing activities need to be performed in order to implement the strategies that have been selected as part of the planning process?
- How can the necessary activities to be divided so that individuals or groups can be assigned responsibility for performing them [that is, organized into separate roles and jobs]?
- Once activities have been grouped into specific jobs, what kind of authority and responsibility should be assigned?

- How and by whom should decisions be made? [Attempt to always and ultimately have one person who is singularly responsible for decisions].
- How specialized should roles be?
- Who should control the work being performed?
- How can communication and coordination among members of the organization be facilitated?
- How can job and role descriptions be developed to take into account both functions and accountabilities?
- How can coordination and communication with the external social environment be facilitated?

Also strive to have:

- Every employee 0ultimately reporting to one person, if possible, and they should know who that person is. Job descriptions are often complained about, but they are useful in specifying who reports to whom.
- Carefully consider the span of control, that is, how many people are reporting to whom. Can each manager really supervise that many people in an effective fashion?
- When done designing the group, always build structure into the new design through the use of organizational charts, job descriptions, policies and procedures that document the design and who is doing what in it.

Guidance on Safe Manning

The Safe Manning, Hours of Work and Watchkeeping Regulations 1997 place clear responsibilities on companies owning or operating UK-registered seagoing ships, and other ships whilst in United Kingdom waters, to ensure that their ships are manned with personnel of appropriate grades who have been properly trained and certificated. The numbers of certificated officers and certificated and non-certificated ratings must be sufficient to ensure safe and efficient operation of the ship at all times. Regulation 14 of SOLAS Chapter V states that all ships to which SOLAS Chapter I applies, (i.e. ships on international voyages - cargo ships of 500 gt or more and all passenger ships,) are required to hold a safe manning document. Owners or operators of cargo ships below 500 gt may also find it advantageous.

The owner or operator of a United Kingdom registered ship is required to make an assessment of the numbers and grades of personnel necessary for safe operation. These should be sufficient to ensure that:

- The required watchkeeping standard can be maintained and that personnel are able to obtain sufficient rest;
- Personnel are not required to work more hours than is safe in relation to the safety of the ship;
- The master and seamen can perform their duties in accordance with the framework of operational guidance in section A-VIII of the STCW Code;
- The master and seamen are not required to work such hours or under such conditions which may be injurious to their health and safety.
- Proposals based on the assessment should be submitted to the Maritime and Coastguard Agency (MCA) which, when satisfied that the proposed manning levels are adequate, will issue a safe manning document.
- Previously, the UK Administration specified minimum numbers of certificated officers and the grades of certificates which should be held for different types of ships and power levels, and in some cases the numbers of ratings. The 1997 Regulations take a less prescriptive approach. The responsibility to ensure that ships are safely, sufficiently and efficiently manned rests with owners and managing operators. Guidance on determining appropriate manning levels is given in Annex 1 of IMO Assembly Resolution A.890(21).

- In order to avoid possible problems at a later stage, owners and operators are recommended to consult with seafarers' representatives and the MCA on their proposed manning when new ship are at the design stage and in advance of registering existing ships in the UK.
- In the event of any disagreement between the owners and official seafarers' representatives regarding manning levels, the MCA will consider any views put forward and may require a revision of the manning levels, if so justified. In such cases, it may be necessary to arrange for some form of practical demonstration of the ability of the crew to carry out the essential tasks in the context of the principles of safe manning. Similarly, in the event of any change in the equipment, construction or use of the ship, which may affect the safe manning level, the owner or operator should make an application for the issue of a new safe manning document.

Specialist Ship Types

- Offshore support vessels present special problems because of the diverse nature of their operations and the conditions under which they are required to operate. Owners are particularly reminded of the restrictions placed on working hours under the Regulations and should set manning levels accordingly.
- Shipowners and operators must ensure that the master, officers and ratings on tankers, and the master, officers, ratings and other personnel on ro-ro passenger ships have completed the training required by the Regulations which is specified in sections A-V /1 and A-V /2 of the STCW Code. All crew members on high speed craft must have completed the training required under the SOLAS High Speed Craft Code, and masters and officers having an operational role must hold a Type Rating Certificate as required by

the SOLAS Code. On passenger ships generally, the need to handle large numbers of passengers unfamiliar with the marine environment must be taken into account in determining manning levels. Personnel should be appropriately trained and certificated and owners and operators must give particularly careful attention to the requirements for minimum numbers of trained crew to take charge of survival craft.

Safe Manning Documents

When the MCA has agreed proposals regarding manning of a particular ship, a safe manning document will be issued for that ship in a format which complies with the requirements of SOLAS 1974, as amended. It should be retained on board and be available for inspection whenever required by an authorised person.

Principles of Sale Manning

Recalling Article 15(j) of the Convention on the International Maritime Organization concerning the functions of the Assembly in relation to regulations and guidelines concerning maritime safety and the prevention and control of marine pollution from ships,

Recalling Also Article 28(a) of that Convention which requires the Maritime Safety Committee to consider, inter alia, the manning of seagoing ships from a safety standpoint,

Noting that safe manning is a function of the number of qualified and experienced seafarers necessary for the safety of the ship, crew, passengers, cargo and property and for the protection of the marine environment,

Recognizing the importance of the requirements of the pertinent IMO instruments as well as those adopted by ILO, ITU and WHO relevant to maritime safety and protection of the marine environment,

Mindful of the provisions of SOLAS regulation V/13 with respect to the issue of an appropriate safe manning document or equivalent as evidence of minimum safe manning,

Being Aware that the ability of seafarers to maintain observance of these requirements is dependent upon their continued efficiency through conditions relating to training, hours of work and rest, occupational safety, health and hygiene and the proper provision of food,

Believing that international acceptance of broad principles as a framework for administrations to determine the safe manning of ships would materially enhance maritime safety and protection of the marine environment.

Having Considered the recommendation made by the Maritime Safety Committee at its seventy-first session,

- Adopts the Principles of safe manning, the Guidelines for the application of principles of safe manning and the Guidance on contents and model form of minimum safe manning document, set out respectively in Annexes 1, 2 and 3 to the present resolution;
- Recommends that Governments, in establishing the minimum safe manning levels for ships flying their countries' flag, observe the Principles set out in Annex 1 and take into account the Guidelines set out in Annex 2;
- Urges Governments to ensure that minimum safe manning documents contain, as a minimum, the information given in Annex 3;
- Urges Further Governments, when exercising port State control functions under international conventions in force with respect to foreign ships visiting their ports, to regard compliance with such documents as evidence that such ships are safely manned;
- Requests the Maritime Safety Committee to keep this resolution under review;
- Revokes resolution A.481(XII).

Annex 1

Principles of Safe Manning

- The following principles should be observed in determining the minimum safe manning of a ship: the capability to:
- Maintain safe navigational, engineering and radio watches in accordance with regulation VIII/2 of the 1978 STCW Convention, as amended, and also maintain general surveillance of the ship;
- Moor and unmoor the ship safely;
- Manage the safety functions of the ship when employed in a stationary or near-stationary mode at sea;
- Perform operations, as appropriate, for the prevention of damage to the marine environment;
- Maintain the safety arrangements and the cleanliness of all accessible spaces to minimize the risk of fire;
- Provide for medical care on board ship;
- Ensure safe carriage of cargo during transit; and
- Inspect and maintain, as appropriate, the structural integrity of the ship; and the ability to:
- Operate all watertight closing arrangements and maintain them in effective condition, and also deploy a competent damage control party;
- Operate all on-board fire-fighting and emergency equipment and life-saving appliances, carry out such maintenance of this equipment as is required to be done at sea, and muster and disembark all persons on board; and
- Operate the main propulsion and auxiliary machinery and maintain them in a safe condition to enable the ship to overcome the foreseeable perils of the voyage.

In applying such principles, Administrations should take proper account of existing IMO, ILO, ITU and WHO instruments in force which deal with:

- Watchkeeping;
- Hours of work or rest;
- Safety management;
- Certification of seafarers;
- Training of seafarers;
- Occupational health and hygiene; and
- Crew accommodation.

The following on-board functions, when applicable, should also be taken into account:

- Ongoing training requirements for all personnel, including the operation and use of fire-fighting and emergency equipment, life-saving appliances and watertight closing arrangements;
- Specialized training requirements for particular types of ships;
- Provision of proper food and drinking water;
- Need to undertake emergency duties and responsibilities; and
- Need to provide training opportunities for entrant seafarers to allow them to gain the training and experience needed.

Annex 2

Guidelines for the application of Principles of Safe Manning

Introduction

- These guidelines should be used in applying the principles of safe manning set out in Annex 1 to this resolution to ensure the safe operation of, and the prevention of pollution from, ships to which article III of the 1978 STCW Convention, as amended, applies.
- The Administration may retain or adopt arrangements which differ from the provisions herein recommended and which are especially adapted to technical developments and to special types of ships and trades.

However, at all times the Administration should satisfy itself that the detailed manning arrangements ensure a degree of safety at least equivalent to that established by these guidelines.

Hours of Work or Rest

- Every company is obliged to ensure that the master, officers and ratings do not work more hours than is safe in relation to the performance of their duties and the safety of the ship. The same responsibility is placed on the master in relation to the members of the ship's complement. Manning levels should be such as to ensure that the time and place available for taking rest periods are appropriate for achieving a good quality of rest. Further guidance about fitness for duty is contained in section B-VIII/1 of the STCW Code.
- A record of the actual hours of work performed by the individual seafarer should be maintained on board, in order to verify that the minimum periods of rest required under relevant and applicable international instruments in force have been complied with.

Determination of Minimum Safe Manning levels

The purpose of determining the minimum safe manning level of a ship is to ensure that its complement includes the grades/capacities and number of persons required for the safe operation of the ship and the protection of the marine environment.

The minimum safe manning level of a ship should be established taking into account all relevant factors, including the following:

- Size and type of ship;
- Number, size and type of main propulsion units and auxiliaries;
- Construction and equipment of the ship;
- Method of maintenance used;

- Cargo to be carried;
- Frequency of port calls, length and nature of voyages to be undertaken;
- Trading area(s), waters and operations in which the ship is involved;
- Extent to which training activities are conducted on board; and
- Applicable work hour limits and/or rest requirements.

The determination of the minimum safe manning level of a ship should be based on performance of the functions at the appropriate level(s) of responsibility, as specified in the STCW Code, which include the following:

- Navigation, comprising the tasks, duties and responsibilities required to:
- Plan and conduct safe navigation;
- Maintain a safe navigational watch in accordance with the requirements of the STCW Code;
- Manoeuvre and handle the ship in all conditions; and
- Moor and unmoor the ship safely;
- Cargo handling and stowage, comprising the tasks, duties and responsibilities required to:
- Plan, monitor and ensure safe loading, stowage, securing, care during the voyage and unloading of cargo to be carried on the ship;
- Operation of the ship and care for persons on board, comprising the tasks, duties and responsibilities required to:
- Maintain the safety and security of all persons on board and keep life-saving, fire-fighting and other safety systems in operational condition;
- Operate and maintain all watertight closing arrangements;
- Perform operations, as appropriate, to muster and disembark all persons on board;

- Perform operations, as appropriate, to ensure protection of the marine environment;
- Provide for medical care on board the ship; and
- Undertake administrative tasks required for the safe operation of the ship;
- Marine engineering, comprising the tasks, duties and responsibilities required to:
- Operate and monitor the ship's main propulsion and auxiliary machinery and evaluate the performance of such machinery;
- Maintain a safe engineering watch in accordance with the requirements of the STCW Code;
- Manage and perform fuel and ballast operations; and
- Maintain safety of the ship's engine equipment, systems and services;
- Electrical, electronic and control engineering, comprising the tasks, duties and responsibilities required to:
- Operate the ship's electrical and electronic equipment; and
- Maintain the safety of the ship's electrical and electronic systems;
- Radiocommunications, comprising the tasks, duties and responsibilities required to:
- Transmit and receive information using the radio equipment of the ship;
- Maintain a safe radio watch in accordance with the requirements of the ITU Radio Regulations and the 1974 SOLAS Convention, as amended; and
- Provide radio services in emergencies;

Maintenance and repair, comprising the tasks, duties and responsibilities required to:

- Carry out maintenance and repair work to the ship and its machinery, equipment and systems, as appropriate to the method of maintenance and repair used.

In addition to the factors and functions in paragraphs, the determination of the minimum safe manning level should also take into account:

- The management of the safety functions of a ship at sea when not under way;
- Except in ships of limited size, the provision of qualified deck officers to ensure that it is not necessary for the master to keep regular watches by adopting a three-watch system;
- Except in ships of limited propulsion power or operating under provisions for unattended machinery spaces, the provision of qualified engineer officers to ensure that it is not necessary for the chief engineer to keep regular watches by adopting a three-watch system;
- The maintenance of applicable occupational health and hygiene standards on board; and
- The provision of proper food and drinking water for all persons on board, as required.

In determining the minimum safe manning level of a ship, consideration should also be given to:

- The number of qualified and other personnel required to meet peak workload situations and conditions, with due regard to the number of hours of shipboard duties and rest periods assigned to seafarers; and
- The capability of the master and the ship's complement to co-ordinate the activities necessary for the safe operation of the ship and the protection of the marine environment.

Responsibilities of Companies

The Administration may require the company responsible for the operation of the ship to prepare and submit its proposal for the minimum safe manning level of a ship in accordance with a form specified by the Administration.

In preparing a proposal for the minimum safe manning level of a ship, the company should apply the principles, recommendations and guidelines contained in this resolution and should be required to:

- Make an assessment of the tasks, duties and responsibilities of the ship's complement required for its safe operation, for protection of the marine environment, and for dealing with emergency situations;
- Make an assessment of numbers and grades/capacities in the ship's complement required for its safe operation, for protection of the marine environment, and for dealing with emergency situations;
- Prepare and submit to the Administration a proposal for the minimum safe manning level based upon the assessment of the numbers and grades/capacities in the ship's complement required for its safe operation and for protection of the marine environment, justifying the proposal by explaining how the proposed ship's complement will deal with emergency situations, including the evacuation of passengers, where necessary;
- Ensure that the minimum safe manning level is adequate at all times and in all respects, including meeting peak workload situations, conditions and requirements, and is in accordance with the principles, recommendations and guidelines contained in this resolution; and
- Prepare and submit to the Administration a new proposal for the minimum safe manning level of a ship in the case of changes in trading area(s), construction, machinery, equipment or operation and maintenance of the ship, which may affect the safe manning level.

Approval by the Administration

A proposal for the minimum safe manning level of a ship submitted by a company to the Administration should be evaluated by the Administration to ensure that:

- The proposed ship's complement contains the number and grades/capacities of personnel to fulfil the tasks, duties and responsibilities required for the safe operation of the ship, for protection of the marine environment and for dealing with emergency situations; and
- The master, officers and other members of the ship's complement are not required to work more hours than is safe in relation to the performance of their duties and the safety of the ship and that the requirements for work and rest hours, in accordance with applicable national regulations, can be complied with.

The Administration should require a company to amend a proposal for the minimum safe manning level of a ship if, after evaluation of the original proposal submitted by the company, the Administration is unable to approve the proposed composition of the ship's complement.

The Administration should only approve a proposal for the minimum safe manning level of a ship and issue accordingly a minimum safe manning document if it is fully satisfied that the proposed ship's complement is established in accordance with the principles, recommendations and guidelines contained in this resolution, and is adequate in all respects for the safe operation of the ship and for the protection of the marine environment.

The Administration may withdraw the minimum safe manning document of a ship if the company fails to submit a new proposal for the ship's minimum safe manning level when changes in trading area(s), construction, machinery, equipment or operation and maintenance of the ship have taken place which affect the minimum safe manning level.

The Administration should review and may withdraw, as appropriate, the minimum safe manning document of a ship which persistently fails to be in compliance with rest hours requirements.

Guidance on Contents and Model from of Minium Safe Manning Document

The following information should be included in the minimum safe manning document issued by the Administration specifying the minimum safe manning level:

- A clear statement of the ship's name, port of registry, distinctive number or letters, IMO number, gross tonnage, main propulsion power, type and trading area and whether or not the machinery space is unattended;
- A table showing the number and grades/capacities of the personnel required to be carried, together with any special conditions or other remarks;
- A formal statement by the Administration that, in accordance with the principles and guidelines set out in Annexes 1 and 2, the ship named in the document is considered to be safely manned if, whenever it proceeds to sea, it carries not less than the number and grades/capacities of personnel shown in the document, subject to any special conditions stated therein;
- A statement as to any limitations on the validity of the document by reference to particulars of the individual ship and the nature of service upon which it is engaged; and
- The date of issue and any expiry date of the document together with a signature for and the seal of the Administration.

It is recommended that the minimum safe manning document be drawn up in the form corresponding to the model given in the appendix to this Annex. If the language used is not English, the information given should include a translation into English.

Manning Arrangements

Employers using offshore manning arrangements will then be liable to pay Class 1 (and indeed Class 1A and Class

1B, as appropriate) where the employee is working wholly or mainly in UK waters. There are defined as A, B, C or D under the Merchant Shipping (Categorisation of Waters) Regulations 1992 and included in the Merchant Shipping Notice 1776(M).

Shipping companies using offshore manning arrangements to engage mariners wholly or mainly outside the UK waters defined continue not to have a UK National Insurance contribution liability. Such employers would include international shipping, most ferries, coastal cargo trade and aggregate carriers operating wholly or mainly outside the specified waters.

Where employers are unclear about the incidence of liability, eg because the pattern of work takes mariners both into and out of the defined waters for various reasons, there will be a clearance procedure operated by contacting the 'Employer Compliance Unit Manager' at the local Tax Office.

In some cases the position will be affected where duties involve travel into the waters of EC/EEA and reciprocal agreement countries.

Designated Person

To ensure the safe operation of each ship and to provide a link between the company and those on board, every company, as appropriate, should designate a person or persons ashore having direct access to the highest level of management. The responsibility and authority of the designated person or persons should include monitoring the safety and pollution prevention aspects of the operation of each ship and to ensure that adequate resources and shore based support are applied, as required.

Master's Responsibility and Authority

The Company should clearly define and document the master's responsibility with regard to:

- Implementing the safety and environmental protection policy of the Company;
- Motivating the crew in the observation of that policy;

- Issuing appropriate orders and instructions in a clear and simple manner;
- Verifying that specified requirements are observed; and
- Reviewing the SMS and reporting its deficiencies to the shore based management.

The Company should ensure that the SMS operating on board the ship contains a clear statement emphasizing the Master's authority. The Company should establish in the SMS that the master has the overriding authority and the responsibility to make decisions with respect to safety and pollution prevention and to request the Company's assistance as may be necessary.

Resources and Personnel

The Company should ensure that the master is:

- Properly qualified for command;
- Fully conversant with the Company's SMS; and
- Given the necessary support so that the Master's duties can be safely performed.

The Company should ensure that each ship is manned with qualified, certificated and medically fit seafarers in accordance with national and international requirements.

The Company should establish procedures to ensure that new personnel and personnel transferred to new assignments related to safety and protection of the environment are given proper familiarization with their duties. Instructions which are essential to be provided prior to sailing should be identified, documented and given.

The Company should ensure that all personnel involved in the Company's SMS have an adequate understanding of relevant rules, regulations, codes and guidelines.

The Company should establish and maintain procedures for identifying any training which may be required in support of the SMS and ensure that such training is provided for all personnel concerned.

The Company should establish procedures by which the ship's personnel receive relevant information on the SMS in a working language or languages understood by them.

The Company should ensure that the ship's personnel are able to communicate effectively in the execution of their duties related to the SMS.

Development of Plans for Shipboard Operations

The Company should establish procedures for the preparation of plans and instructions for key shipboard operations concerning the safety of the ship and the prevention of pollution. The various tasks involved should be defined and assigned to qualified personnel.

Emergency Prep Aredness

The Company should establish procedures to identify, describe and respond to potential emergency shipboard situations.

The Company should establish programmes for drills and exercises to prepare for emergency actions.

The SMS should provide for measures ensuring that the Company's organization can respond at any time to hazards, accidents and emergency situations involving its ships.

Reports and Analysis of Non-Conformities, Accident and Hazardous Occurrences

The SMS should include procedures ensuring that non-conformities, accidents and hazardous situations are reported to the Company, investigated and analyzed with the objective of improving safety and pollution prevention.

The Company should establish procedures for the implementation of corrective action.

Maintenance of the Ship and Equipment

The Company should establish procedures to ensure that the ship is maintained in conformity with the provisions of the relevant rules and regulations and with any additional requirements which may be established by the Company.

In meeting these requirements the Company should ensure that:

- Inspections are held at appropriate intervals;
- Any non-conformity is reported with its possible cause, if known;
- Appropriate corrective action is taken; and
- Records of these activities are maintained.

The Company should establish procedures in SMS to identify equipment and technical systems the sudden operational failure of which may result in hazardous situations. The SMS should provide for specific measures aimed at promoting the reliability of such equipment or systems. These measures should include the regular testing of stand-by arrangements and equipment or technical systems that are not in continuous use.

The inspections mentioned in 10.2 as well as the measures referred to 10.3 should be integrated in the ship's operational maintenance routine.

Documentation

The Company should establish and maintain procedures to control all documents and data which are relevant to the SMS.

The Company should ensure that:

- Valid documents are available at all relevant locations;
- Changes to documents are reviewed and approved by authorized personnel; and
- Obsolete documents are promptly removed.

The documents used to describe and implement the SMS may be referred to as the "Safety Management Manual". Documentation should be kept in a form that the Company considers most effective. Each ship should carry on board all documentation relevant to that ship.

Company Verification, Review and Evalution

The Company should carry out internal safety audits to verify whether safety and pollution prevention activities comply with the SMS.

The Company should periodically evaluate the efficiency and when needed review the SMS in accordance with procedures established by the Company.

The audits and possible corrective actions should be carried out in accordance with documented procedures.

Personnel carrying out audits should be independent of the areas being audited unless this is impracticable due to the size and the nature of the Company.

The results of the audits and reviews should be brought to the attention of all personnel having responsibility in the area involved.

The management personnel responsible for the area involved should take timely corrective action on deficiencies found.

Certification, Verufucation and Control

The ship should be operated by a Company which is issued a document of compliance relevant to that ship.

A document of compliance should be issued for every Company complying with the requirements of the ISM Code by the Administration, by an organization recognized by the Administration or by the Government of the country, acting on behalf of the Administration in which the Company has chosen to conduct its business. This document should be accepted as evidence that the Company is capable of complying with the requirements of the Code.

A copy of such a document should be placed on board in order that the Master, if so asked, may produce it for the verification of the Administration or organizations recognized by it.

A Certificate, called a Safety Management Certificate, should be issued to a ship by the Administration or organization recognized by the Administration. The Administration should, when issuing a certificate, verify that the Company and its shipboard management operate in accordance with the approved SMS.

The Administration or an organization recognized by the Administration should periodically verify the proper functioning of the ship's SMS as approved.

Chapter 7

Shipboard Oil Pollution Emergency Plan

This flow diagram is an outline of the course of action that shipboard personnel should follow in responding to an oil pollution emergency based on the guidelines published by the Organization. This diagram is not exhaustive and should not be used as a sole reference in response. Consideration should be given for inclusion of specific reference to the Plan. The steps are designed to assist ship personnel in action to stop or minimize the discharge of oil and mitigate its effects. These steps fall into two main categories – reporting and action.

- Discharge of Oil Probable or Actual
- Assessment of the Nature of Incident
- Actions required
  – Alert crew members
  – Identity spill source
  – Spill assessment

REPORTING

By Master and/ or Designated Crew Member

When to Report

All probable and actual spills

How to Report

- By quickest means to coastal radio station
- Designated ship movement reporting sta-tion or

- Rescue Co-ordination Centre (at sea)
- By quickest available means to local autho-rities

Who to Report

- Nearest Coastal State Harbour and termi-nal operators (in port)
- Shipowner's manager; P and I insurer
- Head Charterer; Cargo owner
- Refer to contact lists

What to Report

- Initial report (Res. A.851(20))
- Follow-up reports
- Characteristics of oil spilled
- Cargo/ ballast/ bunker dispositions
- Weather and sea conditions
- Slick movement
- Assistance required
  - Salvage
  - Lightening capacity
  - Mechanical equipment
  - External strike team
  - Chemical dispersant/ degreasant

ACTION TO CONTROL DISCHARGE

Measures to minimize the escape of oil and threat to the marine environment

Navigation Measures

- Alter course/ position and/ or speed
- Change of list and/ or trim
- Anchoring
- Setting aground
- Inititate towage

- Assess safe haven require-ments
- Weather/ tide/ swell fore-casting
- Slick monitoring
- Record of events and communications taken

Seamanship Measures

- Safety assessment and pre-caution
- Advice on priority countermeasures/ preventive measures
- Damage stability and stress consideration
- Ballasting/ deballasting
- Internal cargo transfer opera-tions
- Emergency ship-to-ship trans-fers of cargo and/ or bunker
- Set up shipboard response for:
  - Leak sealing
  - Fire fighting
  - Handling of ship-board response equipment (if available)
  - Etc.

Steps to Initiate External Response

- Refer to Costal Port State listings for local assistance
- Refer to ship interest contact list
- External clean-up resources required
- Continued monitoring of activities

Section 2: Reporting Requirements

General

The reporting requirements of this section complies with those of regulation 26 of MARPOL 73/ 78, Annex I.

When the ship is involved in an incident which results in the discharge (or probable discharge) of oil, the Master is obliged under the terms of MARPOL 73/ 78 to report details of the incident, without delay, to the nearest Coastal State by means of the fastest telecommuncation channels available.

The intent of these requirements are to ensure that Coastal States are informed, without delay, of any incident giving rise to oil pollution, or threat of oil pollution, of the marine environment, as well as of assistance and salvage measures, so that appropriate action may be taken.

Without interfering with shipowners' liability, some coastal states consider that it is their responsibility to define techniques and means to be taken against an oil pollution incident and approve such operations which might cause further pollution, i.e. lightening. States are in general entitled to do so under the International Convention relating to Intervention on the High Seas in Cases of Oil Pollution Casualties, 1969.

Reporting Procedures

For easy reference the reporting requirements in the context of this Plan are divided in the following information blocks:

When to report

Taking the summary flowchart as shown on page 6 as a basic guide into consideration reports are necessary in the following cases:

Actual Discharge

The Master is obliged to report to the nearest Coastal State whenever there is a discharge of oil re-sulting

- From damage to the ship
- From damage to the ship's equipment
- For the purpose of securing the safety of a ship or saving life at sea
- During the operation of the Ship in excess of the quantity or instanteneous rate permitted under the present Convention

Probable Discharge

The Master is obliged to report even when no actual discharge of oil has occured but there is a pro-bability that one could.

However, as it is not practible to lay down precise definitions of all types of situations involving probable discharge of oil which would warrant an obligation to report the Master is obliged to judge by himself whether there is such a probability and whether a report should be made.

Therefore, it is recommended that, at least, the following events

- Damage, failure or breakdown which affects the safety of the ship (e.g. collision, grounding, fire, explosion, structural failure, flooding, cargo, cargo shifting etc.)

or

- Failure or breakdown of machinery or equipment which results in impairment of the safety of navi-gation (e.g. failure or breakdown of steering gear, propulsion, electrical generating system, essen-tial shipborne navigation aids etc.) are carefully considered by the Master – taking into account the nature of the damage failure or break- down of the ship, machinery or equipment as well as the ship's location, proximity to land, weather, state of the sea and traffic density – as cases in which a probable discharge of oil is most likely.

If in doubt, the Master should always make a report in cases aforementioned.

In all cases the Authorities should be kept informed by the Master as how the situation progress and be advised when all threat of pollution has passed.

Information Required

As required in article 8 and Protocol I of MARPOL 73/ 78 Convention the Master or other persons having charge of the ship should report the particulars of any pollution incident.

In this context the International Maritime Organization (IMO), in 1997, adopted Resolution A. 851 (20) "General Principles for Ship Reporting Systems and Ship Reporting Requirements, including Guidelines for Reporting Incidents involving Dangerous Goods, Harmful Substances and/ or Marine Pollutants".

The intent of the Resolution aforementioned is to enable Coastal States and other interested parties to be informed, without delay, of any incident giving rise to oil pollution, or threat of oil pollution, of the marine environment, as well as of assistance and salvage measures, so that appropriate action may be taken.

Nothing in this chapter relieves the Master in using sound judgement to make sure that any incident or propable discharge of oil is reported as quick as possible in the prevailung situation.

When transmitting initial reports to the authorities of the nearest Coastal State the Master or other persons dealing with such a transmission should take note of Resolution A. 851 (20).

Especially, the format of the initial report as well as supplementary of follow-up reports should conform with the guidance contained in Res. A. 851 (20). All reporting whether initial or follow-up, should follow IMO's reporting format as outlined below and should contain the following information:

Label	Function	Eexplanation
A	Ship	Name, call sign and nationality
B	Date and time (UTC) of event	A 6-digit group giving day of month (first two di-gits), hours and minutes (last four digits)
C	Position	A 4-digit group giving latitude in degrees and mi-nutes suffixed with N or S, and a 5-digit group gi-ving longitude in degrees and minutes suffixed with E or W

D	Position	True bearing (first 3 digits) and distance (state distance) in nautical miles from clearly identified landmark (state landmark)
E	True course	A 3-digit group
F	Speed at time of incident	In knots and tenths of knots as a 3-digit group
L	Route information	Details of intended track
M	Radio communications	Full details of radio stations (names) and frequen-cies being guarded
N	Time (UTC) of next report	A 6-digit group as under BB above
P	Cargo on board: can be included in „RR„ as relevant	Type(s) and quantity(ies) of cargo/ bunker on board and brief details of any dangerous cargoes as well as harmful substances and gases that could endager persons or the environment
Q	Defects or damage or defencies or other limitations	Brief details of conditions of the ship as relevant; ability to transfer cargo/ ballast/ bunker fuel
R	Description of pollution or possi-ble overboard discharge	Brief details of pollution; this should include the type(s) of fuel oil, an estimate of the quantity discharged, whether the discharge is continuing, the cause of the discharge and, if possible, an estimate of the movement and area of slick
S	Weather conditions	Brief details of weather and sea conditions prevai-ling including wind force and direction and relevant swell details
T	Ship's representative and/ or owner	Name, adress, telex and telephone number of the ship´s owner and representative (charterer, mana-ger or operator of the ship or their agents)

U	Ship's size and type	Details of length, breadth and type of ship as well as draught
X	Miscellaneous and additional information	Any other information including relevant details such as brief details of incident, need for outside assistance, action being taken to limit further discharge; details of any personnel injuries su-stained, details of P and I Club and local correspon-dent.

All follow-up reports by the Master should include information relevant to the Coastal State Authorities to keep them informed as the incident develops.

Follow-up reports should include information on any significant changes in the ship's condition, the rate of release and spread of oil, weather and sea conditions and clean-up activities underway.

In this context details of bunker disposition, condition of any empty tanks and nature of any ballast carried are information needed by those involved in order to assess the threat posed by an actual or probable discharge of oil from the damaged ship.

Who to Contact

The Master is responsible for reporting any incident involving an actual or probable discharge of oil.

Taking into consideration the summary flowchart shown the Master of the ship involved in any kind of an actual or probable discharge of oil, cases of which are defined under SECTION 2 (sub-paragraph 2.2.1.1 and 2.2.1.2) of this Plan should report details on the incident immediately.

Nothing in this chapter relieves the Master from using sound judgement to make sure that any inci-dent is reported as quick as possible in the prevailing situation.

Coastal State Contacts

In order to expedite response and minimize damage from an oil pollution incident at sea, it is essential that appropriate Coastal States be notified without delay.

In this context the use of the list of agencies or officials of Administrations responsible for receiving and processing reports (so called "Focal Points") as developed by the Organization (IMO) in confor-mity with article 8 of the Convention is recommended.

Such a list is shown under App. 2.

Operational Spills

Operational Spill Prevention

Crew members shall maintain a close watch for the escape of oil during bunker operations. Prior to bunker transfer the competent crew members should mobilize the oil spill equipment, as far as available on board, and place it close to the planned operation, e.g. along the railing on the side at which bunker operation takes place.

Before bunker handling commences, all deck scuppers and open drains must be effectively plugged. Accumulations of water should be drained periodically and scupper plugs replaced immediately after the water has run off. Any free floating oil or oil droplets should be removed prior to draining.

Bunker tanks which have been topped up should be checked frequently during the remaining bunker operations to avoid an overflow. Unless there are permanent means for retention of any slight leakage at ship/ shore connections for bunker transfer, it is essential that a drip tray is in place to catch any leaking oil.

The removed bunker oil and the used clean-up material should be retained on board in proper containment units until it can be discharged to a reception facility.

Pipeline Leakage

If a leakage occurs from a pipeline, valve, hose or metal arm, operations through that connection should be stopped immediately until the cause has been ascertained and the defect remedied.

Defective pipe sections should be isolated. Affected sections should be drained down to an available empty or slack tank. If a leakage occurs from a hydraulic pipeline, operations should be stopped immediately.

Initiate clean-up procedures

The removed bunker oil and the used clean-up material should be retained on board in proper containment units until it can be discharged to a reception facility. Inform in line with Section 2 all parties interested about Pipeline Leakage and the actions taken so far.

Tank Overflow

If there is a tank overflow all bunker operations should be stopped immediately and should not be restarted until the fault has been rectified and all hazards from the released oil have been eliminated.

If there is any possibility of the released oil or oil vapours entering an engine room intake appropriate preventive steps must be taken quickly. Promptly shift bunker oil from the tank overflowed to an available empty or slack tank or prepare pump(s) or transfer the excess ashore.

Initiate clean-up procedures

The removed bunker oil and the used clean-up material should be retained on board in proper containment units until it can be discharged to a reception facility. Inform in line with Section 2 all parties interested about Tank Overflow and actions taken so far.

Hull Leakage

Identify leaking tank; consider diver if necessary and possible. Reduce level in tank in question well below sea level. If it is not possible to identify the leaking tank, reduce level in all tanks in vicinity. In this case give careful consideration to hull stress and stability. If there is a spillage due to suspected hull leakage reduce the head of bunker and promptly transfer the bunker oil to an available empty or slack tank or, if berthed, discharge ashore in suitable barges/ tanks.

Inform in line with Section 2 all parties interested about Hull Leakage and the actions taken so far.

Spills caused by Equipment in Machinery Spaces

If operational oil spills are caused by a failure of equipment in machinery spaces any further operations of this equipment should be stopped immediately or measures are to be taken to avoid an oil spill.

Such equipment may be:

- Oily-water separating equipment or oil filtering equipment to deoil bilge water from the engine room bilges
- Valves in pipes connecting ballast/ bilge systems
- Cooling pipes in oil cooler systems
- Gearing of bow thrusters
- Stern tubes

The removed bunker oil and the used clean-up material should be retained on board in proper containment units until it can be discharged to a reception facility.

Spills Resulting From Casualties

In the event of a casualty the Master's first priority is to ensure the safety of the ship's personnel, and to initiate actions which may prevent escalation of the incident and marine pollution.

Ship grounded /Stranded

The Master's priority should be to ensure that he as soon as possible receives detailed information about the damage that the ship has been sustained, in order to determine remedial action to be taken for ensuring the safety of the ship and its crew.

Furthermore, the Master should also consider

- Danger to the ship's complement if the ship should slide off grounding site
- Danger of ship being shattered by heavy seas or swell
- Health hazards to the ship's crew and surrounding population due to release of oil or other hazardous substances in dangerous concentrations
- That fires may start due to released flammable substances and uncontrolled ignition sources
- Should the damage which the ship has sustained be of such an extent that the stability cannot be computed on board, the Master should seek assistance according to subparagraph 3.6

Also, the ship's Master shall take into account the following considerations:

- Is the vessel constantly being struck in the seaway?
- Is the vessel exposed to torsion?
- Is there a large difference in the tidal rangers at the grounding site?
- Are there strong tidal currents in the grounding area?
- May the vessel drift further up on the shore, due to high tides, wind and waves?

Prevention of Fire and Explosion

If the ship is aground and therefore cannot manoeuvre, all possible sources of ignition should be eliminated and action taken to prevent flammable vapours from entering the machinery spaces or the accommodation.

Extension of Hull Damage / Containment System Failure

First, a visual inspection should be carried out. Check for visible oil along hull or in wake of the ship during day time. At night a stick with white cloth (or sheet of sorbent) around it may be lowered into the water alongside the ship to check for oil leakages.

All ballast/ bunker tanks to be sounded (ullage),

All other compartments which may have contact with the sea should be sounded to ensure that they are intact. Soundings of ballast tanks/ bunkers tanks are to be compared with last soundings to check for possible leaks. Sounding to be taken around the ship establish the ship's position on the grounding area. When the ship is aground, due regards should be given to the indiscriminate opening of ullage plugs, sighting ports etc. as loss of buoyancy could be the result of such actions.

Any list of the ship shall be noted and included in the report for assistance.

Procedures to Reduce or Stop Outflow of Oil

The Master should assess the possibility of damage to the environment and whatever action can be taken to reduce further damage from an oil release, such as:

- Transfer of bunkers internally provided shipboard piping system is in an operational condition
- If the damage is fairly limited and restricted, i.e. to one or two tanks, consideration should be given to transfer of bunkers internally from the damaged tank(s) to intact tanks, taking into account the impact on the ship's overall stress and stability
- Isolate damaged/ penetrated bunker tank(s) hermetically to ensure that hydrostatic pressure in tanks remains intact during tidal changes
- Evaluate possibility of pumping water into a damaged tank inorder to form a water bottom stopping the outfow of oil
- Evaluate the necessity of transferring bunkers to barges or other ships and request such assistance accordingly
- Evaluate the possibility of additional release of oil.

In case of large differences between the tidelevels, the Master should try to isolate the damaged tank(s) to reduce additional loss of bunker oil.

Refloating by Own Means

The Master should also evaluate the question of refloating the vessel by own means. Before such an attempt is made, it must be determined:

- Wether the ship is damaged in such a way that it may sink, break up or capsize after getting off
- Wether the ship after getting off may have manoeuvering problems upon leaving the dangerous area by own means
- Whether machinery, rudder or propeller are damaged due to grounding or may be damaged by trying to get off ground by own means
- Whether the ship may be trimmed or lightened sufficiently to avoid damage to other tanks in order to reduce additional pollution from oil/ bunker spillage
- Weather evaluation: whether there is time/ reason to await improvements in weather or tide.

Chapter 8

Marine Communication

A simulator for shipboard radio frequency interference, intended to be used in the characterization of UHF satellite communications terminals such as the AN/WSC-3 and AN/SSR-1, has been developed. A physical-statistical model for shipboard interference, based on Middleton's model for urban noise, is given. The model developed incorporates the relevant physical aspects of the various possible interferers and postulates a statistical framework in which these signals are inserted.

A simulator based on the developed model was built to serve as a tool for study of the effects of the various interferers upon shipboard satellite communications systems. The simulator is capable of generating 10 types of complex emitters and of providing linear and nonlinear processing of them. It is also capable of generating a PSK modulated test signal for performance measurements of UHF terminals. Results of performance measurements are presented. These results demonstrate the ability of the simulator to reproduce the shipboard electromagnetic environment.

SHIP DISTRESS AND SAFETY COMMUNICATIONS ENTER NEW ERA

Ship distress and safety communications enter a new era today with the full implementation of the Global Maritime Distress and Safety System (GMDSS) - an integrated communications system using satellite and terrestrial radiocommunications to ensure that no matter where a ship is in distress, aid can be dispatched.

The GMDSS was developed by the International Maritime Organization (IMO), the specialized agency of the United Nations with responsibility for ship safety and the prevention of marine pollution, in close co-operation with the International Telecommunication Union (ITU) and other international organizations, notably the World Meteorological Organization (WMO), the International Hydrographic Organization (IHO) and the COSPAS-SARSAT partners.

Under the GMDSS, all passenger ships and all cargo ships over 300 gross tonnage on international voyages have to carry specified satellite and radiocommunications equipment, for sending and receiving distress alerts and maritime safety information, and for general communications. The regulations governing the GMDSS are contained in the International Convention for the Safety of Life at Sea (SOLAS), 1974, which has been ratified by 138 countries, covering 98.36 percent of the world merchant shipping fleet by tonnage.

The GMDSS requirements are contained in Chapter IV of SOLAS on Radiocommunications and were adopted in 1988. The requirements entered into force on 1 February 1992 but provided for a phase-in period until 1 February 1999.

IMO Secretary-General Mr. William A. O'Neil said today that the full implementation of the GMDSS is an important date in maritime history, coming as it does almost exactly 100 years after the first use of wireless technology to aid a ship in distress.

Italian engineer Guglielmo Marconi invented radio in 1895 and the first use of wireless in communicating the need for assistance came on 3 March of 1899 when a freighter rammed the East Goodwin Lightship which was anchored ten miles offshore from Deal in the Straits of Dover off the south east coast of England. A distress call was transmitted by wireless to a shore station at South Foreland and help was dispatched.

Mr. O'Neil said: " A century ago, Marconi was demonstrating his new wireless telegraphy system and it was soon clear how valuable wireless would be in saving lives at sea. But wireless had its limitations, notably in terms of the distance that could be covered.

"In the 1960s, IMO recognised that satellites would play an important role in search and rescue operations at sea and in 1976 the Organization established the International Maritime Satellite Organization, which later changed its name to the International Mobile Satellite Organization (Inmarsat) to provide emergency maritime communications. In 1988, IMO's Member States adopted the basic requirements of the global maritime distress and safety system or GMDSS as part of SOLAS.

"Now, as we approach the 21st century, we have in place an integrated communications system which should ensure that no ship in distress can disappear without trace, and that more lives can be saved at sea."

Under the GMDSS requirements, all ships were required to be equipped with NAVTEX receivers, to automatically receive shipping safety information, and satellite emergency position-indicating radiobeacons (EPIRBs) from 1 August 1993. Ships built on or after 1 February 1995 have been required to be fitted with all applicable GMDSS equipment. Ships built before that date were given until 1 February 1999 to comply fully with all the GMDSS requirements.

The GMDSS communications system under SOLAS complements the International Convention on Maritime Search and Rescue (SAR), 1979, which was adopted to develop a global SAR plan, so that no matter where an incident occurs, the rescue of persons in distress will be coordinated by a SAR organization and, where necessary, by co-ordination between neighbouring SAR countries.

IMO's senior technical body, the Maritime Safety Committee (MSC), has divided the world's oceans into 13 search and rescue areas, in each of which the countries concerned have delimited search and rescue regions for which they are responsible. Provisional search and rescue plans for all of these areas have been completed, with the final area, the Indian Ocean, finalised at a conference held in Fremantle, Western Australia in September 1998.

Mr. O'Neil said that with the completion of the SAR plans and the full implementation of the GMDSS, seafarers and ships' passengers could feel safer and more secure at sea.

"In a sense, we have the hardware in place. From today all ships required to do so must comply with the GMDSS and for that we can thank the pioneers who, three decades ago, first saw the possibilities offered by satellite communications to save lives at sea, and then had the vision and imagination to develop a cohesive and coherent global maritime distress and safety system.

"But we should also think about the software - the people who operate the ships, and the people onshore who will monitor and act on distress calls. We must ensure that the people who will be responsible for operating GMDSS equipment are adequately trained, to avoid false distress alerts. Having all the correct equipment on board ship in an emergency situation may be of little use if people on board the ship have not been through the required emergency drills.

"A little more than a century ago, before the the advent of wireless communication, ships were cut off at sea, dependent on passing vessels for help in the event of an emergency. Now we can communicate with a ship anywhere in the world - but this does not mean we can be complacent. We should do our utmost to prevent emergencies from happening in the first place, by developing a safety culture and ensuring all maritime safety and pollution prevention regulations are fully implemented. And we should be trained and prepared for dealing with any eventual emergency.

Shipboard Cable

Shipboard Cables which are made of ethylene-propylene-rubber (EPR), silicone rubber (SR) insulation and metal wire armor are manufactured as the wires of power, signal controlling and communications on shipboard. In order to continue highest achievement of serving the industry, our company with vast experiences and high standards manufacture the national standard cables. Hua Eng Wire and Cable Co., Ltd continually researches to develop and introduce the highest technology and latest available. The following you will find the specification of the ordinary standard of JIS C 3410 which describes our cable's construction and current rating. Furthermore, our company also manufacture the IEC 92-3, MIL-2194, MIL-C-915, IEEE-45 and another types of shipboard cables. We sincerely hope to hear from you and very near future and continue to maintain our business with you.

Symbols of Number of Core and Main Use			
S	Single core for lighting and power	**F**	Four core for lighting and opwer
D	Double core for lighting and power	**M**	Multi-core for control and signal
T	Three core for lighting and power	**TT**	Telephone and instrumentation

Insulation (1)	**Outer covering**	**Armoring (2)**	**Protective covering**	**Otherwise**
P EP rubber	**Y** PVC sheath	**C** Steel wire braid	**Y** PVC protective covering	**S** Common shield
SR Silicone rubber	**NPCP** sheath	**B** Copper alloy wire braid		**-S** individual core or pair shield
T PVC	**D** Braid			

EX DPYCY-14

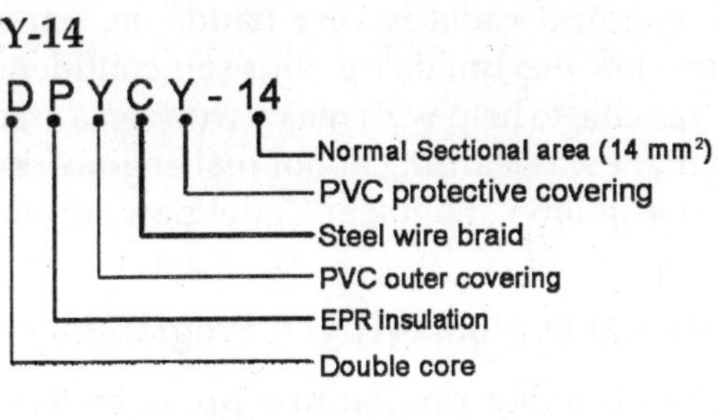

Chapter 9

Training on Board Ships and the Ship Company

The SSTG provides comprehensive training programmes to assist engineer cadets in qualifying for a range of different qualifications enabling them to develop a career as an engineer officer. This includes programmes for Higher National Diplomas (HND) and Undergraduate Degrees.

An engineer officer is responsible for the safe and efficient running of all the technical aspects of the vessel. The officer works as part of a sophisticated management team, and has responsibilities that extend to the supervision of the engine room ratings.

"I enjoyed my training. It was only natural, I suppose, to have preferred the time spent at sea to the time in college because that is where I would be when I finished training. The work of an engineer cadet is very hands on, particularly on smaller ships, but this builds up your self confidence. On one occasion I was able to help with major work on a cracked sump - I felt then that I was learning about real engineering and also gaining responsibility." Engineer Cadet now serving at sea as a junior officer

Higher National Diploma (HND) Programmes

The HND training programme provides thorough and stimulating training in all key skills that you will require in order to fulfil the considerable demands that an engineer officer will encounter whilst working on board ship. These programmes typically take approximately three years to complete and alternate between training at sea and on-shore.

During the college phases academic and theoretical studies are completed together with practical and simulator training, making for a stimulating and rewarding learning environment. In the sea phases of training on board ship you will learn quickly how to become competent with the very specific demands that will be placed on you, and become comfortable with the adjustments you will need to make to enjoy life at sea. During the sea phases you will receive practical and professional training that follows a structured training portfolio to provide evidence of your growing competence and skills.

To give you an idea of how an HND training programme may work we have given an example here of a typical programme framework. Exactly how your own HND programme will look will depend upon the specific programme you are following, and the exact combination and duration of sea and college phases are likely to vary accordingly.

Example of an HND Programme

Phase	Duration	Content
1	26 weeks	STCW BASIC TRAINING Commence Level 3 Underpinning Knowledge.
2	6 months	INITIAL SEA PHASE Commence Portfolio. Introduction to Engineroom watchkeeping.
3	40 weeks	REVIEW OF PRACTICAL TRAINING completed during phase 2. Complete Level 3 Underpinning Knowledge Commence HND studies.
4	6 months	FINAL SEA PHASE Completion of Portfolio and watchkeeping service.
5	26 weeks	COMPLETION OF HND MARINE ENGINEERING Advanced practical training covering: • Level 3 assessment • MCA Oral Examination.

Successful completion of the HND programme for an Engineer Cadet leads to the award of the following, as appropriate to the course you are taking.

- Maritime and Coastguard Agency certificate of competency as an unrestricted Engineer Officer Of The Watch.
- Higher National Diploma (HND) in Marine or Mechanical Engineering.
- National/Scottish Vocational Qualification Level 3 in Marine Engineering Operations.

The HND incorporates most of the academic studies for Second Engineer and Chief Engineer Certificates of Competency which will provide you with a good basis for continuing to develop your career.

The HND also provides you with an opportunity for you to continue further studies later in your career in order to gain a degree in your relevant discipline.

Undergraduate Degree Programmes

The undergraduate programme incorporates all the components for the candidate to qualify for a Marine or Mechanical Engineering degree. The programme takes four years and is the equivalent of three years spent at university and one year at sea completing all the required practical training necessary to qualify for the certificate of competence.

This programme can be followed by candidates wishing to achieve a degree as well as the professional qualifications enabling them to serve at sea. Alternatively, candidates may chose this route whose aim is to move into a role in one of the many associated maritime sectors ashore but where the knowledge gained by qualifying as an engineer officer will be valuable experience in the shore career. Typically this might include roles within the fields of marine insurance and finance, legal work and arbitration, and other economic, operational or other management fields.

The academic work in a maritime studies degree incorporates all of the necessary studies to qualify for the unrestricted Engineer Officer of The Watch certificate as well as additional studies about the maritime sector which provides for a fascinating and relevant understanding of how the industry operates. These additional subjects include shipping policy; international maritime and trading law; maritime economics; ship design and survey; ship operations and management; marine engineering; maritime safety and management; environmental protection; port operations; and business management.

During the sea periods on board ship, practical and professional training is undertaken following a structured training portfolio to provide evidence of your growing competence and skills.

Successful completion of the degree programme leads to the award of the following:

- Maritime and Coastguard Agency certificate of competency as an unrestricted Engineer Officer Of The Watch
- B.Sc.(Hons) Degree in Marine or Mechanical Engineering
- National/Scottish Vocational Qualification Level 3 in Marine Engineering Operations.

The degree incorporates most of the academic studies for Second Engineer and Chief Engineer Certificates of Competency which will provide you with a good basis for continuing to develop your career.

Modern ships are technologically advanced and require seafarers to have a wide range of expertise, depending on their position on board, from basic practical to complex management, technical and organizational skills. There is no bar to women serving at sea, and there are female captains and chief engineers.

The Ship's Company

There are normally two main departments on board - deck and engine room. Ships carrying passengers also have a hotel services department.

The deck department is concerned with the overall operation of the ship, responsibilities including navigation, communications, cargo or other ship operation, stability, maintenance, and safety.

The engine room department is responsible for all technical services including main engine propulsion, other plant and machinery, electrical generation, maintenance, cargo or other ship operation, and safety.

The number in a ship's company varies according to the size and type of ship and area of operation, and may range between as few as six and up to twenty-five or more. These numbers will be significantly higher on passenger ships and ferries in all departments but particularly in the hotel services department, depending on the number of passengers carried. Irrespective of the size of the ship's company, the structure of the various departments follows the same pattern, an example of which is shown in the table below. Limited numbers of other specialist personnel may also be carried. The smaller the total numbers on board, the more inter-departmental work activity occurs.

The Deck Department

The ship's master is the highest ranking officer on board and has overall command and responsibility for the vessel, its crew, any passengers and cargo. The Master (Captain) maintains the ship's records, has responsibility for accounting and bookkeeping, and receives and implements instructions from the operating company of the vessel. The Master will also take command of the vessel in inclement weather or any other emergency, and in crowded or narrow waters.

The First Mate has direct responsibility for all deck operations including cargo storage and handling, deck maintenance, and deck supplies. He or she will also assign and monitor watches and will be on smaller ships the medical officer.

The Second Mate is the ship's navigation officer and has the responsibility for maintaining charts and monitoring the navigation equipment on the bridge.

The Third Mate assists other officers as directed and has immediate responsibility for the regular maintenance of emergency survival equipment including lifeboats and life rings.

Ratings

The Deck Department is manned by ratings which include the Boatswain (Bosun), who has direct responsibility for supervising the seamen working within the department. The Able Seaman's (AB) duties include standing watch, during which he or she will steer the vessel and generally assist the mate on watch, and undertake maintenance and docking duties. An Ordinary Seaman (OB) is an apprentice AB and will assist the AB's bosun and officers and undertake activities to ensure the vessel is kept orderly.

The Engine Room Department

"Before I went on board I expected the ships to be very large - you see films made on huge ferries and cruise liners and expect them all to be like that, and of course they are not. The reality wasn't a problem - as soon as I got down to the engine room the whole thing came alive for me. It is very exciting to be an engineer." Engineer Cadet now serving at sea as a junior officer

The Engine Room Department falls under the overall charge of the Master but with day-to-day immediate duties as below.

Chief Engineer

The head of the Engineering Department, the Chief Engineer has overall responsibility for the functioning of the engine room and all mechanical equipment on the ship. He or she will keep records of all engine parts and repairs, be responsible for calculating fuel and water consumption and requirements, and coordinate operations with the shoreside port engineer.

Second Engineer

Directly involved in engine maintenance and assigns duties to engine room ratings and work priorities according to the Chief's requirements.

Third Engineer

Assists other engineer officers as required.

Some ships will have a dedicated electrical officer responsible for all the electrical and electronic control systems and equipment

Ratings

The Engine Department may also have a small number of ratings who will have direct responsibility for general routine maintenance and other tasks associated with some of the more basic technical systems.

Larger vessels will also have crew with specific responsibilities for communication and catering.

Chapter 10

Skills and Techniques

Method and System for Marine Vessel Tracking System

A marine ship tracking system automatically and accurately monitors ship movements utilizing a limited number of reports from a marine ship and is easily installed and operated. Ships utilizing the marine ship tracking system periodically transmit reports to a remote tracking center. A ship sends a report to the remote tracking center when there is a significant change in the ship's movement or position, or if a predetermined amount of time has elapsed since the ship last sent a report to the remote tracking center. The report includes current ship information, such as current position and current movement information. Because the ship sends a report each time a significant change in movement occurs, the remote tracking center may accurately extrapolate the position of the ship between the transmissions of the reports. In this manner, the remote tracking center may retain an accurate history of the ship's position and movements at all times.

Control of Motions and Response

Control of motions and response of ships at speed is of vital importance for passenger, Ro-Ro, navy and container ships. Development of such systems require monitoring of waves, different type of sensors, ship operational limits of the ships and advanced control systems. Marintek is working together with a number of international partners within this area; Lockheed Martin, Nigel Gee, Pacific Marine Design and others. Marintek is the coordinator of an EU-financed project together with several partners within hull monitoring.

In order to investigate the performance and the operational limits for ship using control systems etc., a simulator is necessary. The simulator is used for:

- Safety analysis such as failure mode and effect analysis (FMFA)
- Development of control systems (algorithms, sensor integration, redundancy)
- Training
- Documentation of the entire control system

The simulator is based on accurate ship models, sensor models and control software developed in cooperation with NTNU. New methods of determining ship models parameter will be focused on in this strategic R and D programme.

Complex Operations and Fleet Planning

Marintek represents the Royal Norwegian Navy on:

- NATO, Specialist Team on Naval Ship Manoeuvrability.
- NATO, Specialist Team on Simulation-Based Design and Virtual Prototyping.

These groups are developing NATO standards for simulating major operations at sea. Such operations often include large and small vessels, helicopters and submarines. The simulation models will be used both for training, as decision-support systems and in the design phase. Each individual country is responsible for its own module in the system.

Marintek has adapted the NATO standard for simulating ship operations.

Another objective is to develop tools for both optimal utilisation of a large number of ships, helicopters etc., fleet planning as well as for different types of operations; rescue, emergency, offshore marine operations.

In Congested Waters

Raining and decision-support systems for use on board ship and ashore, i.e. "shore-based remote pilotage", will improve safety in approaches and harbours where safety margins are marginal. With support provided by the Norwegian Shipowners' Association, Marintek is developing a system for Jebsen Management AS for the approaches to Svea Mine in Svalbard. Requirements regarding safe operation in these waters are stringent, because special attention needs to be paid to the environment.

The individual components of such a system consist of:

- Vessel simulation models (vessel, propeller/rudder/thruster, effects of depth, etc.).
- Description of local waters, including depths, currents, wind, waves, etc.
- Modelling of the local geography, i.e. approaches and harbour conditions, including weather and visibility.

The system will be designed in such a way that it is updated and modified via measurements of individual on-board parameters during operation. Simulation models can also be installed and utilized in full-scale training simulators.

Electronic charts are well on the way to becoming standard equipment on board ship. The decision-support, training and remote pilotage system employs this technology to improve the competence of the navigator in handling his own vessel, navigating in particular waters and improving navigational safety.

Modelling assistance provided by tugs is another module of the system.

Damaged Ship

Better systems for emergency planning and rescue operations are necessary.

Several accidents at sea, collisions and groundings have demonstrated the need for better knowledge and understanding about the loads, floating capability and strength of ships which is partly damaged. Along the Norwegian coast alone 3-4 groundings occurred last winter resulting in oil pollution and extensive rescue operations.

In Port and Harbours

Ship handling in harbours and ports is of increasing importance with increased traffic, larger vessels and demand for shorter turn-around time as speed increases.

High precision positioning and tracking system require exact knowledge about the ship behaviour in shallow water, wind, effects of other nearby ships/structures and the propulsion/thruster systems.

Marintek is involved in a project together with Fjellstrand AS and Rolls Royce Marine for developing a part docking system for their high speed ferry "Ferry Cat".

Exploitation of the Oceans

Exploitation of the ocean requires efficient and accurate manoeuvring of surface ships combined with different underwater systems, ROVs, trawls etc. Marintek is working close together with the SINTEF Fisheries and Aquaculture and NTNU in developing models for simulation of such systems for exploitation of marine resources. Such systems have to be very accurate and is often very complex and advanced, requiring the best knowledge within hydrodynamics and cybernetics.

Offshore Marine Operations

There is quite a variety of offshore marine operations requiring the best knowledge within hydrodynamic of ships and other structures, cybernetics and structural engineering.

Offshore ships for cable-laying, intervention, crane operations, pipeline laying etc are highly specialised working platforms for which motions as well as accurate and reliable positioning and tracking are crucial.

Together with the shipbuilders and suppliers we will develop the next generation of systems to increase cost-effectiveness and reliability for offshore marine operations.

Strategic University Program on Marine Cybernetics

Marine Cybernetics is a multidisciplinary education, research and development programme launched by Faculty of Marine Technology and Department of Engineering Cybernetics at NTNU addressing modelling and control of marine dynamical systems. The main objective of the research programme is to create the necessary expertise and the technology basis to support the new advances on marine control system design for marine operations and sea transportation.

Currently, 12 Ph.D. students are involved in research on active control of wave induced motion of fast ferries, underway replenishment and fleet control, control of flow and vortex induced vibrations of risers for deep water installations, control of seismic cables, propulsion and energy optimality in dynamic positioning and control trawl system in fisheries. The research fields in Marine Cybernetics are closely linked to the research topics addressed in Nautilus. In addition, the simulation and testing infrastructure developed through the Nautilus program will be extensively used in the research at NTNU. Key personnel in Marine Cybernetics group at NTNU are also involved in the Nautilus programme.

Chapter 11

Sail Training

From its modern interpretations to its antecedents when maritime nations would send young naval officer candidates to sea , sail training provides an unconventional and effective way of building many useful skills on and off the water. Through the unique environment of the sea, contemporary sail trainees learn that what they are doing is important and that their efforts are essential to the operation and safety of the ship.

The daily operation of a sailing ship can be tough and is not for everyone. Airplanes and automobiles have replaced ships and boats as the primary mode of transportation, a fact lamented by educators such as Kurt Hahn. Many people today are more familiar with the loops and turns of a roller coaster than the rhythmic motion of the sea. Those who overcome their initial consternation will find that wind can be harnessed through physics. Engineering is used to manipulate the sails with various lines and tackle while math and geography are used to calculate the current location and potential destinations.

Surrounded on all sides by the marine environment, whales and dolphins are frequent visitors and the vessel is itself, a lesson in history. Halyards and sheets require teamwork and discipline to set and, in the isolation created by the sea, the vessel and the crew must become self-sufficient by necessity. Each individual must act independently yet interdependently to cope with the physical, mental and emotional challenges they are faced with.

Background

By 1900 most commercial sailing vessels were struggling to turn a profit in the face of competition from more modern steam ships which had become efficient enough to steam shorter great circle routes between ports instead of the longer trade wind routes used by sailing ships.

Sailing ship owners used a variety of methods to compete. Ships were built larger to carry bulk cargoes more efficiently, their rigs were simplified to reduce manning costs and speed was no longer a premium. Owners shipped cargoes that were non-perishable so that their date of arrival (which steam ships had started to guarantee) were of less importance. Finally as the Panama Canal was opened, sailing ships were used in parts of the world where steam ships still found it hard to operate: principally on the Chilean Nitrate Trade (for fertilizers and explosive production in Europe) and on the Australian grain trade. Both Chile and Australian ports were difficult to supply with coal for steamships to refuel.

The end of the First World War saw a brief return to profitability as all ship types were in scare supply due to wartime losses but that boom became bust as many new steam ships were built to replace the sailing ships that were lost.

Genesis in the 1930's

While many countries of the world operated sailing ships as training vessels for officers in their Merchant Marine in the 1920's and 30's, several sailing ship owners such as Carl Laeisz and Gustav Erickson determined that there was still a profit to be made from the last of the sailing ships.

Erickson purchased existing ships that required the minimum of capital investment and repaired them with parts cannibalised from other ships. Identifying the bulk cargo routes that would still offer paying freights, he manned the ships with a smattering of paid experienced officers.

The deckhands were apprentices from steamship lines and other adventurous youth who had all paid a premium to sail while being trained. These crews were considered trainees and were the first formalization of sail trainers with crew drawn from members of the public who just went for the adventure, as opposed to a career.

With manning costs netted out on Erickson's balance sheet, the ships continued to return a paper profit. However Erickson was under no illusions as to the long term profitability of his venture, which depended on ignoring the depreciation on his ships and a shrinking supply of sound hulls and rigs. The company would use their profits to diversify into steam after World War II.

While the shipping companies of Erickson and F. Laeisz gradually turned to steam, the next generation of captains were crawling through up the hawse hole and taking command of their own vessels, redefining sail training as a purely educational endeavour with trainees as the cargo.

From 1932 through 1958, Irving Johnson and his wife Electa "Exy" Johnson circumnavigated the world 7 times with amateur youth crews on board their vessels named *Yankee*. Over the years, their voyages were featured in books they authored, and in National Geographic magazines and TV specials like *"Irving Johnson, High Seas Adventurer"*. Their archives are at Mystic Seaport, Connecticut.

Australian Alan Villiers purchased the old school ship *George Stag* from Denmark, in 1934. Renaming her the *Joseph Conrad*, he sailed her round the world with no paying cargo and a crew of youth who had paid to be there. He also took as many non-paying youth as he could afford to fit in the budget, those he considered at risk on the streets of their inner cities and in need of what was then called "character building". These trip were the genesis of current modern sail training, using manually operated ships and the harsh discipline imposed by the sea to further personal development and taking those disadvantaged by circumstance to benefit from the experience.

By the end of World War II, the numbers of traditionally rigged sailing ships left were dwindling and public interest waned. The loss of the *Pamir* in 1957 and the *Albatross* in 1961 drew further ill will and seemed to signal the end of an era.

Modern Sail Training

In what was conceived to be last great gathering of square-riggers under sail, Bernard Morgan and Greville Howard persuaded a number of ship owners to join together in a sort of farewell salute in 1956, organizing a race from Torbay on the South Coast of England to race informally across the Bay of Biscay to Lisbon in Portugal. Five square rigged school ships entered the race, Denmarks' Danmark, Norway's Christian Radich and Sorlandet, Belgium's Mercator and Portugal's first Sagres.

The event proved to be anything but a funeral procession as the race would fire the imagination of owners and "owners to be" and the vessels would meet again the following year and every year since in an annual series that would astonish its original organizers today. Old vessels were saved or repaired and new purpose built sail training vessels were commissioned. With renewed interest in the age of sail, national sail training associations affiliated to Sail Training International (STI) (formerly "Sail Training Association") were organized and large summer events find upwards of 100 ships racing across the oceans.

Crew exchanges allow young people from one country to sail with those from another. Long before the end of the Cold War, ships from Russia and Poland joined the International Fleet in 1974 and put the totalitarianism of their regimes behind them. A limited exchange between the East and West was initiated and they put their respective backgrounds behind them, common sailors joined together by the brotherhood of the sea.

One of the largest of the affiliate organizations of the STI is the American Sail Training Association (ASTA). Founded in 1973 with a handful of vessels, it has since grown to encompass an international organization with more than 250 tall ships representing 25 different countries.

While the summer race series are the pinnacle of the sail training experience, most maritime nations have government, private and charitably funded ships preserving the ways of seamen from a time gone by, helping the youth and the "young at heart" find themselves and working somewhere off their coasts on short trips year round.

Square rigged seamanship was almost in danger of becoming a lost art. As the 1997 restoration of the USS Constitution neared completion, the United States Navy called on the crew of HMS Bounty to train her sailors how to sail the vessel as she was originally intended to.

Many boats are historical vessels and replicas which require coordinated manual labor to sail, operating in the original tradition proposed by Alan Villiers and Irving Johnson such as the Picton Castle while others are purpose built educational platforms carrying out scientific research under sail such as the Robert C. Seamans and the Corwith Cramer of the Sea Education Association.

Sail training has proven useful in providing at-risk youth with real life challenges that develop the knowledge, skills and attitudes needed to live healthy, productive lives. As the crew of the Irving Johnson and the award winning program at the Los Angeles Maritime Institute like to say "We do not train youth for a life at sea... we use the sea to educate youth for life".

Vessel Classifications

Tall ships have been found to be effective platforms for sail training as they combine many elements fundamental to sail training. A "Tall ship" is not a strictly defined type of vessel. "Tall ship" is commonly used today to define a large, traditionally rigged vessel, whether or not is it technically a ship. For example, the USCGC Eagle is technically a barque and not a fully rigged ship. A tall ship is usually defined by the topmast and topsails she carries as opposed to the modern high aspect ratio rigs and marconi mains carried by the sloops and yawls seen in every harbor today.

For the purpose of classification and race rating, the STI divides Tall ships into the following classes :

Class A: All vessels over 160 feet in length overall, regardless of rig, and square rigged vessels over 120 feet in length.

Class A; Division II: All square rigged vessels less than 120 feet in length.

Class B: Fore-and-aft rigged vessels between 100 feet and 160 feet in length

Class C: All other fore-and-aft rigged vessels at least 30 feet long at the waterline.

The United States Coast Guard classifies vessels based on their intended use and structure, prescribing requirements for captain and crew manning, waters the vessel may operate in, number of passengers allowed and minimum safety equipment required.

With the exception of uninspected vessels, all such vessels are inspected annually and issued a Certificate of Inspection (COI) which must be displayed on the vessel and spells out the requirements that vessel must maintain.

Sailing School Vessel (SSV): Inspected under Title 46, Subchapter R of the Code of Federal Regulations (CFR). An SSV is a vessel of less than 500 gross tons carrying six or more sailing school students or instructors, primarily propelled by sail, and operated by a nonprofit educational organization exclusively for the purpose of sailing education.

Passenger Vessel: Certified according to the size and number of passengers (not engaged in educational activities or in the operation of the vessel) carried under Title 46 of the CFR.

Subchapter C: Uninspected vessels which operate with no more than six passengers.

Subchapter T: Small passenger vessels of under 100 gross tons that carry more than six passengers and are required to pass regular USCG inspection of the ship and all onboard equipment.

Subchapter K: Small passenger vessels of under 100 gross tons that carry more than 150 passengers and are required to pass regular USCG inspection of the ship and all onboard equipment.

Subchapter H: Passenger vessels of more than 100 gross tons that carry passengers for hire and are required to pass regular USCG inspection of the ship and all onboard equipment.

Attraction Vessel: Certification is required whenever a vessel is open to public boarding or conducts dockside programs. The vessel may be permanently moored to a pier, or it may be certified under one or more of the above subchapters, but the Attraction Vessel COI certifies its safety for dockside and visitation only.

Oceanographic Research Vessel (ORV): Certified under Subchapter U of Title 46 of the CFR. An ORV is a vessel employed exclusively in either oceanographic (saltwater) or limnologic (freshwater) instruction and/or research, and is not necessarily equipped for passengers or other non-professionals.

Pros and cons of sail training

Sail training is not intended to be a vacation. The sea has always been associated with some element of risk and if one were looking to stay warm and dry, then a cruise ship would tend to be more appropriate. Sail training is about the excitement and challenge of undertaking a journey the natural maritime elements. Whether they be bitter cold winds turning droplets of spray into needles piercing the exposed flesh of the helmsmen's hands and face or the hot tropical sun beating down upon the sailors hour after hour as the sails hang limply as they hope and pray for the faintest breath of wind, challenge and adventure tends to be the primary goal of those interested in sail training.

With many options out there, it can be a difficult choice with interests as varied as marine biology and adventure travel; day, week, or school semesters in length and races across the Atlantic to afternoon cannon battles out in the harbour.

While one can generally expect to handle lines and standing watch, vessels differ as to the degree of responsibility as well as whether the vessels is underway day and night or if the voyage ventures from harbor to harbor and on anchor each night.

Space is also limited and most accommodations involve less privacy than one may be accustomed with. Dormitory style living is most common with several people sharing a single cabin and personal space limited to the area occupied by the individual bunk. For this reason, it is advised that luggage be limited to only what is necessary and carried in duffel bags or soft sided luggage as one may end up having to sleep with a hard suitcase in their bunk as there is no place else to put it.

Cost of delivery needs also to be borne in mind. There are few tall ships around the world, for example, that survive without government subsidy, donors, sponsors or rich clientele.

Chapter 12

Marine Corps

The Marine Corps serves as an amphibious force in readiness. Today, it has three primary areas of responsibility riginally introduced under the National Security Act of 1947:

- The seizure or defense of advanced naval bases and other land operations to support naval campaigns
- The development of tactics, technique, and equipment used by amphibious landing forces
- "Such other duties as the President may direct."

The quoted clause, while seemingly a consequence of the President's position as Commander in Chief, is a codification of the expeditionary duties of the Marine Corps. It derives from similar language in the Congressional Acts "For the Better Organization of the Marine Corps" of 1834, and "Establishing and Organizing a Marine Corps" of 1798. In 1951, the House of Representatives Armed Services Committee called the clause "one of the most important statutory–and traditional–functions of the Marine Corps." It noted that the Corps has more often than not performed actions of a non-naval nature, including its roles in the War of 1812, World War I, the Korean War, its famous actions at Tripoli and Chapultepec, and their numerous counterinsurgency and occupational duties in Central America and East Asia. These actions are not accurately described as support of naval campaigns nor as amphibious warfare. Their common thread is that they are of an expeditionary nature - using the mobility of the Navy to provide timely intervention in foreign affairs on behalf of American interests.

In addition to its primary duties, the Marine Corps has missions in support of the White House and State Department. President Jefferson dubbed the Marine Band the "President's Own" for its role of providing music for state functions at the White House. In addition, Marines guard presidential retreats, including Camp David and the Marine unit HMX-1 provides helicopter service to the President. By authority of the 1946 Foreign Service act, Marines of the Marine Corps Security Guard provide security for American embassies, legations, and consulates at over 110 State Department posts overseas.

Historical Mission

At its founding, the Marine Corps was composed of infantry serving aboard naval vessels, responsible for the security of the ship and her crew by conducting offensive and defensive combat during boarding actions, and defending the ship's officers from mutiny; to the latter end, their quarters on ship was often strategically positioned between the officers' quarters and the rest of the vessel. They were also responsible for manning raiding parties. The Marine Corps' role has since expanded significantly. As the importance of its original naval mission declined with changing naval warfare doctrine and the professionalization of the Naval service, the Corps adapted by focusing on what were formerly secondary missions ashore.

The Advanced Base doctrine of the early 20th century codified their combatant duties ashore, outlining the use of Marines in the seizure of bases and other duties on land to support naval campaigns. The Marines would also develop tactics and techniques of amphibious assault on defended coastlines in time for use in World War II. Its original mission of providing shipboard security finally ended in the 1990's, when the last Marine security detachments were withdrawn from U.S. Navy ships.

Capabilities

While the Marine Corps does not employ any unique combat arms, it, as a force, has the unique ability to rapidly deploy a combined-arms task force to almost anywhere in the world within days. The basic structure for all deployed units is a Marine Air-Ground Task Force (MAGTF) that integrates a ground combat component, an air component, and a combat service support component under a common command element. While the creation of joint commands under the Goldwater-Nichols Act has improved interservice coordination between the U.S. military services, the Marine Corps' ability to permanently maintain integrated multi-element task forces under a single command provides a smoother implementation of combined-arms warfare principles.

The close integration of disparate Marine units stems from an organizational culture centered around the infantry. Every other Marine capability exists to support the infantry. Unlike many Western militaries, the Corps remained conservative against theories proclaiming the ability of new weapons to win wars independently. For example, Marine Aviation has always been focused on close air support and has remained largely uninfluenced by airpower theories proclaiming that strategic bombing can singlehandedly win wars.

This focus on the infantry is matched with the notion that "every Marine is a rifleman," emphasizing the infantry combat abilities of every Marine. All enlisted Marines receive training first and foremost as a rifleman; all officers receive training as infantry platoon commanders. The value of this culture has been demonstrated many times throughout history. At Wake Island, when all the Marine aircraft were shot down, their pilots continued the fight as riflemen, leading supply clerks and cooks in a final defensive effort.

The amphibious assault techniques developed for World War II evolved with the addition of air assault and maneuver warfare doctrine, into the current "Operational Maneuver from the Sea" doctrine of power projection from the seas. The Marines are credited with the development of helicopter insertion doctrine, and were the earliest in the American military to widely adopt maneuver warfare principles, which emphasize low-level initiative and flexible execution. As a result, a large degree of initiative and autonomy is expected of junior Marines, particularly the NCOs (Corporals and Sergeants) as compared to many other military organizations. The Marine Corps pushes authority and responsibility downward to a greater degree than the other services. Flexibility of execution is implemented via an emphasis on "commander's intent" as a guiding principle for orders - specifying the endstate but leaving open the method of execution.

The Marine Corps relies upon the Navy for sealift to provide its rapid deployment capabilities. In addition to basing a third of the Marine Corps Operating Forces in Japan, Marine Expeditionary Unit (MEU)'s, a smaller MAGTF, are typically stationed at sea. This allows them the ability to function as first responders to international incidents. The U.S Army now maintains light infantry units capable of rapid worldwide deployment, though they do not match the combined-arms integration of a MAGTF, nor have the logistical train that the Navy provides. For this reason, the Marine Corps is often assigned to non-combat missions such as the evacuation of Americans from unstable countries, and humanitarian relief of natural disasters. In larger conflicts, the Marines act as a stopgap, to get into and hold an area until larger units can be mobilized. It performed this role in World War I, the Korean War, and Operation Desert Storm, where Marines were the first significant combat units deployed from the United States and held the line until the country could mobilize for war.

World War I

In World War I, battle-tested, veteran Marines served a central role in the U.S. entry into the conflict. Unlike the U.S. and British armies, the Marine Corps had a deep pool of officers and NCO's with battle experience, and experienced a relatively smaller expansion. Here, the Marines fought their celebrated battle at Belleau Wood, then the largest in the history of the Corps; it created the Marines' reputation in modern history. Rallying under the battle cries of "Retreat? Hell, we just got here!" (Captain Lloyd Williams) and "Come on, you sons of bitches, do you want to live forever?" (GySgt. Dan Daly), the Marines drove German forces from the area. While its previous expeditionary experiences had not earned it much acclaim in the Western world, the Marines' fierceness and toughness earned them the respect of the Germans, who rated them of storm-trooper quality. Though Marines and American media reported that Germans had nicknamed them "Teufel Hunden" or "Devil Dogs", there is no evidence of this in German records. Nevertheless, the name stuck. The Marine Corps had entered the war with 511 officers and 13,214 enlisted personnel and, by November 11, 1918, had reached a strength of 2,400 officers and 70,000 men.

Between the World Wars, the Marine Corps was headed by Commandant John A. Lejeune. Under his leadership, the Marine Corps presciently studied and developed amphibious techniques that would be of great use in World War II. Many officers, including LtCol Earl Hancock "Pete" Ellis foresaw a pacific war with Japan and took preparations for such a conflict. While stationed in China, then LtCol. Victor H. Krulak observed Japanese amphibious techniques in 1937. Through 1941, as the prospect of war grew, the Marine Corps pushed urgently for joint amphibious exercises, and acquired amphibious equipment such as the Higgins boat which would prove of great use in the upcoming conflict.

World War II

In World War II, the Marines played a central role in the Pacific War; the Corps expanded from two brigades to two corps with six divisions, and five air wings with 132 squadrons. In addition, 20 Defense Battalions and a Parachute Battalion were set up. The battles of Guadalcanal, Tarawa, Saipan, Iwo Jima, and Okinawa saw fierce fighting between U.S. Marines and the Imperial Japanese Army.

During the battle of Iwo Jima, photographer Joe Rosenthal took the famous photo Raising the Flag on Iwo Jima of five Marines and one Navy corpsman raising the American flag on Mt. Suribachi. Secretary of the Navy James Forrestal, who had come ashore earlier that day to observe the progress of the troops, said of the flag raising on Iwo Jima, "...the raising of that flag on Suribachi means a Marine Corps for the next five hundred years." The acts of the Marines during the war added to their already significant popular reputation, and the USMC War Memorial in Arlington, Virginia was dedicated in 1954. By the war's end, the Corps had grown to include six divisions, five air wings and supporting troops totaling about 485,000 Marines. Nearly 87,000 Marines were killed or wounded during World War II and 82 received the Medal of Honor.

Despite Secretary Forrestal's prediction, the Corps faced an immediate institutional crisis following the war. Army generals pushing for a strengthened and reorganized defense establishment also attempted to fold the Marine mission and assets into the Navy and Army. Drawing on hastily assembled Congressional support, the Marine Corps rebuffed such efforts to dismantle the Corps, resulting in statutory protection of the Marine Corps in the National Security Act of 1947. Shortly after, in 1952, the Douglas-Manfield Bill afforded the Commandant an equal voice with the Joint Chiefs of Staff on matters relating to the Marines, and established the structure of three divisions and air wings that remains today. This allowed the Corps to permanently maintain a division and air wing in the Far East and participate in various small wars in Southeast Asia - in the Tachen Islands, Taiwan, Laos, Thailand, and South Vietnam.

Korean War

The Korean War (1950 - 1953) saw the hastily formed Provisional Marine Brigade holding the defensive line at the Pusan Perimeter. To execute a flanking maneuver, General Douglas McArthur called on Marine air and ground forces to make an amphibious landing at Inchon. The successful landing resulted in the collapse of North Korean lines and the pursuit of North Korean forces north near the Yalu River until the entrance of the People's Republic of China into the war. Chinese troops surrounded, surprised and overwhelmed the overextended and outnumbered American forces. However, unlike the Eighth Army, which retreated in disarray, the 1st Marine Division regrouped and inflicted heavy casualties during their fighting withdrawal to the coast. Now known as the Battle of Chosin Reservoir, it entered Marine lore as an example of toughness and resolve. Marines would continue a battle of attrition around the 38th Parallel until the 1953 armistice. The Korean War saw the Marine Corps expand from 75,000 regulars to a force, by the end of the conflict in 1953, of 261,000 Marines, most of whom were reservists. 30,544 Marines were killed or wounded during the war and 42 were awarded the Medal of Honor.

Vietnam War

The Marines also played an important role in the Vietnam War at battles such as Da Nang, Hué City, and Khe Sanh. The Marines operated in the northern I Corps regions of South Vietnam and fought both a constant guerilla war against the NLF and an off and on conventional war against NVA regulars. Marines also conducted the less well-known Combined Action Program that implemented unconventional techniques for counter insurgency warfare. The Marine presence was withdrawn in 1971, but returned briefly in 1975 to evacuate Saigon and attempt to rescue the crew of the Mayagüez. Vietnam was the longest war for the Marine Corps; at its end 13,091 Marines were killed in action and 51,392 wounded, and 57 Medals of Honor were awarded. Due to rotation policies, more Marines served in Vietnam than World War II.

Returning from Vietnam, the Marine Corps hit one of the lowest points in its history with high rates of courts-martial, non-judicial punishments, unauthorized absences, and outright desertions. The re-making of the Marine Corps began in the late 1970s when policies for discharging inadequate Marines were relaxed, leading to the removal of the worst performing ones. Once the quality of new recruits started to improve, the Marine Corps began reforming its NCO corps, a vital element in the functioning of the Marine Corps.

Post Vietnam and Pre-9/11

After Vietnam, the Marines resumed their expeditionary role, participating in the invasion of Grenada (Operation Urgent Fury) and the invasion of Panama (Operation Just Cause). On October 23, 1983, the Marine headquarters building in Beirut, Lebanon was bombed, causing the highest peacetime losses to the Corps in its history (220 Marines and 21 other service members of the 24th MAU were killed) and leading to the American withdrawal from Lebanon. 1990 saw Marines of the Joint Task Force Sharp Edge save thousands of lives by evacuating the British, French and American Nationals from the violence of the Liberian civil war. During the Persian Gulf War (1990–1991), Marine task forces formed the initial core for Desert Shield, while U.S. and Coalition troops mobilized, and later liberated Kuwait in Operation Desert Storm. U.S. Marines participated in combat operations in Somalia (1992–1995) during Operations Restore Hope, Restore Hope II, and United Shield to provide humanitarian relief.

Global War on Terrorism

Marines of the 15th Marine Expeditionary Unit and 26th Marine Expeditionary Unit were the first conventional forces into Afghanistan in support of Operation Enduring Freedom in November of 2001. Since then Marine battalions and squadrons have been rotating through, engaging Taliban and Al Queda forces. Most recently, the Marines have served prominently in Operation Iraqi Freedom. I MEF along with the Army's 3rd Infantry Division spearheaded the 2003 invasion of Iraq. During the occupation of Iraq, Marines spearheaded both assaults on the city of Fallujah in April and November 2004.[35]and continue to operate in the Al Anbar province in western Iraq.

Marine Corps Personnel

Commandants

The Commandant of the Marine Corps is the highest-ranking officer of the Marine Corps, though he may not be the senior officer in time and grade. He is the symbolic and functional head of the Corps, and holds a position of very high esteem among Marines. The commandant has the US Code Title 10 responsibility to man, train, and equip the Marine Corps. He does not serve as a direct battlefield commander. The Commandant is a member of the Joint Chiefs of Staff, and reports to the Secretary of the Navy.

The current and 33rd Commandant of the Marine Corps is General Michael W. Hagee, who assumed the command in January 2003. As of October 2005, Marine Generals Peter Pace (Chairman of the Joint Chiefs of Staff) and James L. Jones (Commander of the United States European Command; NATO Supreme Allied Commander, Europe; and a former commandant of the Marine Corps) are senior in time in grade to the commandant. President Bush has nominated LtGen. James T. Conway to succeed Hagee as the 34th Commandant of the Marine Corps. Conway is currently the JCS Director of Operations (J-3). The nomination was confirmed by the Senate on August 2, 2006. Before assuming his new post, Conway will be promoted to General.

Rank Structure

As in the rest of the U.S. military, (with the exception of the Air Force, which does not have Warrant Officers) ranks fall into one of three categories: commissioned officer, warrant officer, and enlisted, in decreasing order of authority. To standardize compensation, each rank is assigned a pay grade. The following tables list the rank, abbreviation, paygrade, and insignia of each rank.

Commissioned Officers

Commissioned Officers are distinguished from other officers by their commission, which is the formal written authority, issued in the name of the President of the United States, that confers the rank and authority of a Marine Officer. Commissioned officers carry the "special trust and confidence" of the President of the United States. Commissioned officer ranks are further subdivided into Generals, field-grade officers, and company-grade officers.

Commissioned Officer Rank Structure of the United States Marine Corps			
Generals			
General (Gen) O-10	**Lieutenant General (LtGen) O-9**	**Major General (MajGen) O-8**	**Brigadier (BGen) O-7**
☆☆☆☆	☆☆☆	☆☆	☆
Field-grade Officers			
Colonel (Col) O-6	Lieutenant Colonel (LtCol) O-5	Major (Maj) O-4	
Company-grade Officers			
Captain (Capt) O-3	First Lieutenant (1stLt) O-2	Second Lieutenant (2ndLt) O-1	

Warrant Officers

Warrant Officers provide leadership and skills in specialized fields. Unlike most other militaries, the American military confers commissions on its Warrant Officers, though they are generally not responsible for leadership outside of their specialty. Warrant officers come primarily from the senior Non-Commissioned Officer ranks.

A Chief Warrant Officer, CWO2-CWO5, serving in the MOS 0306 "Infantry Weapons Officer" carries a special title, "Marine Gunner" (not a rank). A Marine Gunner replaces the Chief Warrant Officer insignia on the left collar with a bursting bomb insignia. Other warrant officers are sometimes informally also referred to as "Gunner" but this usage is not correct.

Warrant Officer Rank Structure of the United States Marine Corps				
Warrant Officer (WO-1) W-1	Chief Warrant Officer-2 (CWO-2) W-2	Chief Warrant Officer-3 (CWO-3) W-3	Chief Warrant Officer-4 (CWO-4) W-4	Chief Warrant Officer-5 (CWO-5) W-5

Enlisted

Enlisted Marines in the paygrades E-1 to E-3 are "non-noncommissioned officers" or simply "non-rates" and make up the bulk of the Corps' ranks. Although they don't technically hold leadership ranks, the Corps' ethos stresses leadership among all Marines and junior Marines are often assigned responsibility normally reserved for superiors. Those paygrades of E-4 and E-5 are considered non-commissioned officers (NCOs). They primarily supervise junior Marines and act as a vital link with the higher command structure, ensuring that orders are carried out correctly. Marines E-6 and higher are considered Staff Non-Commissioned Officers (SNCOs), charged with supervising NCOs and acting as enlisted advisors to the command.

The E-8 and E-9 levels each have two ranks per pay grade, each with different responsibilities. Gunnery Sergeants (E-7) indicate on their annual evaluations, called "fitness reports", or "fitreps" for short, their preferred promotional track: Master Sergeant or First Sergeant. The First Sergeant and Sergeant Major ranks are command-oriented, with Marines of these ranks serving as the senior enlisted Marines in a unit, charged to assist the commanding officer in matter of discipline, administration and the morale and welfare of the unit. Master Sergeants and Master Gunnery Sergeants provide technical leadership as occupational specialists in their specific MOS. First Sergeants typically serve as the senior enlisted Marine in a company, battery or other unit at similar echelon, while Sergeants Major serve the same role in battalions, squadrons or larger units.

The Sergeant Major of the Marine Corps is a unique rank conferred on the senior enlisted Marine of the entire Marine Corps, personally selected by the Commandant of the Marine Corps. The Sergeant Major of the Marine Corps wears unique chevrons with the Eagle, Globe and Anchor at the center.

Forms of Address

Marines address all enlisted personnel by rank, and all Commissioned officers with "sir" or "ma'am". Warrant

Officers, regardless of rank, are addressed as "Warrant Officer" or "Gunner", although this latter usage is improper unless the Warrant Officer holds the Military Occupational Specialty of Infantry Weapons Officer (MOS 0306). However, during recruit training, recruits are indoctrinated to address drill instructors as "sir". Unlike the Army, ranks containing "Sergeant" are always addressed by their full rank and never shortened to simply "Sergeant"

Informally, some enlisted ranks have commonly used nicknames, though they are not official and technically improper. For instance, a Master Sergeant is commonly called "Top," and a Master Gunnery Sergeant is "Master Guns" or "Master Gunny." A First Sergeant is always referred to by his/her proper rank. A Gunnery Sergeant is typically called "Gunny," and (much less often) "Guns." Likewise, Lance Corporals are often referred to (derisively) as "Lance Coolies", "Lance Coconuts", "Lance Criminals" or some other derivative. They are not usually called by rank due to their status as "non-NCOs", or "non-rates." The rank of Sergeant is never referred to as "Sarge."

Initial Training

Officers

Every year, approximately 1600 new Marine officers are commissioned, and 38,000 recruits accepted and trained. Commissioned officers are commissioned mainly through one of three sources: Naval Reserve Officers Training Corps (NROTC), Officer Candidate School (OCS) – including the Platoon Leaders Class (PLC) and Officer Candidates Class (OCC) – or the United States Naval Academy (USNA).

Following commissioning, all Marine commissioned officers, regardless of accession route or further training requirements, attend The Basic School at Marine Corps Base Quantico, Virginia. There, they spend six months learning to command a rifle platoon. The Basic School, for second lieutenants and warrant officers learning the art of infantry and combined arms warfare, is an example of the Corps' approach to furthering the concept that "Every Marine is a rifleman."

Enlisted

Enlisted Marines attend boot camp, at either Marine Corps Recruit Depot (MCRD) San Diego or Marine Corps Recruit Depot Parris Island, just outside Beaufort, South Carolina. Women only attend the Parris Island depot, in the Fourth Recruit Training Battalion, while males who train at Parris Island comprise the First through Third Battalions. Historically, the Mississippi River served as the dividing line which delineated who would be trained where. More recently, the recruiting district system has been implemented resulting in a more even distribution of male recruits between the two MCRD facilities. Marine recruit training is the longest among the American services; it is 13 weeks long, compared to the Army's 9 weeks.

Enlisted Marines then attend School of Infantry training at Camp Geiger or Camp Pendleton, generally based upon where the Marine received their recruit training. Infantry Marines begin their Military Occupational Specialty (MOS) training immediately with the Infantry Training Battalion (ITB), while all other Marines train with the Marine Combat Training (MCT) Battalion for 22 days, learning common infantry skills, before continuing on to their MOS schools.

Chapter 13

Onboard Training and Challenges

It is difficult to overstress the importance of on-board training for seafers. To learn effectively, one should be as near the real experience as it is poosible to get. That is why on board training is so important for the seafer to develop his competency.

Safety Challenges

The Maritime Safety Committeee (MSC) at its 81st session in May 2006 completed its major work programme item on passenger ship safety, which has based its guiding philosophy on the premise that the regulatory framework should place more emphasis on the prevention of a casualty from occurring in the first place and that future passenger ships should be designed for improved survivability so that, in the event of a casualty, persons can stay safely on board as the ship proceeds to port. A number of amendments to the SOLAS Convention were approved for adoption at MSC 82 in November-December 2006.

It was noted that, with regard to the five pillars of the guiding philosophy for the Committee's passenger ship safety initiative, the following have been achieved since the work was initiated in 2000:

Prevention: Amendments to SOLAS and the STCW Conventions and supporting guidelines that focus on fire prevention, navigation safety, training and contingency planning.

Improved survivability: Amendments to SOLAS chapters II-1 and II-2 and supporting guidelines that focus on essential system redundancy, management of emergencies and casualty mitigation.

Regulatory flexibility: Amendments to SOLAS chapters II-1 and III and supporting guidelines that focus on promoting, through rigorous evaluation and approval procedures, the regulatory approval of new safety technologies and arrangements.

Operations in areas remote from SAR facilities: Action taken to develop amendments to SOLAS chapter III and supporting guidelines that will focus on reducing the time it takes to recover persons from survival craft and the water; supporting guidelines approved on external support from SAR Authorities, as well as guidance to assist seafarers taking part in SAR operations.

Health safety and medical care: Supporting guidelines that focus on establishing medical safety programmes and a revised Guide on Cold Water Survival.

Royal Caribbean's flagship Voyager of the Seas is no ordinary ship. At 142,000 gross tons, she currently holds the title of the world's largest cruise ship.

Imagine the Eiffel Tower in Paris tipped on its side, and you have some idea of her length.

With a capacity of around 1,800 crew and over 3,100 passengers, she can carry the population of a small town.

She boasts the highest "space-per-guest" ratio in the cruise market today and fully embraces the new concept of "the ship is the destination" with such innovative recreational features as an ice rink, a street fair and even an artificial rock-face for budding mountaineers.

Ships such as this have broken the boundaries of convention in terms of their concept, their design and their sheer size. So many things distinguish cruise ships from other ship types but a key factor in their very conception is that they create their own market.

Whereas containerships, for instance, are built in response to their owners' perceptions of the market's requirement, cruise ship owners create a concept and then set out to sell it.

Safety, of course, is a vital concern for passenger ship designers and operators. These vessels have the highest of profiles and their success could be undermined entirely if the public were to lose confidence in them.

Although it cannot be denied that a number of incidents in recent years have indicated the vulnerability of these ships, it is also true that overall, their safety record is good. By and large, they avoid the worst excesses of the weather. Passengers demand that they should do so and a typical power installation capable of providing 25-knots enables them to outrun a hurricane.

But while the modern cruise giants have the power and speed to dodge the weather, they are particularly vulnerable to fire. Every passenger is a potential ignition source and the hotel services clearly have an inherent risk.

Prompted by a concern that the trend toward ever larger vessels could lead to new giants of the cruise world which might pose safety-related questions unforeseen by existing regulations, the then IMO Secretary-General William O'Neil took a personal initiative to raise the issue during the 72nd meeting of the Maritime Safety Committee (MSC) in May 2000.

As a result, the MSC agreed to undertake a global consideration of the safety issues pertaining to these ships and a working group on large passenger-ship safety began work at the next session of the Committee in November-December 2000, to review the current safety regime as it relates to large passenger ships.

What emerged is from IMO was a plan for a body of work that will constitute one of the largest ever investigations into the safety-related aspects a particular ship type ever carried out. The guiding philosophy of the work hinges on the following five elements.

- The regulatory framework should place more emphasis on the prevention of a casualty from occurring in the first place.
- Future large passenger ships should be designed for improved survivability so that, in the event of a casualty, persons can stay safely on board as the ship proceeds to port.
- The regulatory framework should permit alternative designs and arrangements in lieu of the prescriptive regulations, provided that at least an equivalent level of safety is achieved.
- Large passenger ships should be crewed, equipped and have arrangements to ensure the safety of persons on board for survival in the area of operation, taking into account climatic conditions and the availability of SAR functions.
- Large passenger ships should be crewed and equipped to ensure the health safety, medical care and security of persons on board until more specialized assistance is available.

These five elements spawned a host of specific tasks and objectives, which have been built into a thoroughgoing review of the existing safety regime as it applies to these ships. Following work in the Radiocommunications, Search and Rescue (COMSAR), Ship Design and Equipment (DE), Fire Protection (FP), Safety of Navigation (NAV), Stability, Load Lines and Fishing Vessel Safety (SLF) and Standards of Training and Watchkeeping (STW) Sub-Committees between 2000-2004, the MSC agreed at its 79th session in December 2004 that as many of the issues discussed under the agenda item "Large Passenger Ship Safety" applied equally to all passenger ships, the agenda item should be renamed "Passenger Ship Safety". The Committee approved a revised work plan for passenger ship safety and the revised guiding philosophy, strategic goals and objectives.

The revised guiding philosophy for future work on passenger ship safety is based on the premise that the regulatory framework should place more emphasis on the prevention of a casualty from occurring in the first place and that future passenger ships should be designed for improved survivability so that, in the event of a casualty, persons can stay safely on board as the ship proceeds to port.

The unique circumstances of the cruise industry encourage ship designers to seek the key selling points that will make their creation somebody's dream holiday destination.

Passengers' demands for comfort, space and sheer prestige, coupled with economies of scale, mean that the quest for size is likely to continue.

IMO's work is aimed at ensuring that, while this buoyant sector of the shipping industry continues to expand and push at the boundaries of convention, the key issues of safe design and operation can keep pace.

Chapter 14

Protection and Safety of Passenger

SAFETY TRAINING MANUAL

The RVOC Safety Training Manual is comprised of fourteen chapters written to provide guidance and heighten awareness of both personal safety and vessel safety for seamen and scientists aboard UNOLS vessels. This chapter contains selected material from the Safety Training Manual and is oriented towards the research party member.

Oceanographic research vessels are unique; they are away from homeport for extended periods, operate independently-often in remote areas away from shipping lanes-and travel great distances. For all these reasons, safety should be a personal issue with each crew member and researcher on board.

This supplement is an overview of the entire manual and has been prepared to provide researchers and new crew members with a "smorgasbord" of safety information that they may digest in a relatively short period of time.

This supplement is provided so that you can easily digest many important factors that will soon become part of your everyday life. It lists the more common causes of accidents and provides the basic tenets of accident prevention. It further highlights key areas of seamanship, deck systems, lifesaving and survival procedures, fire prevention and control, health and medical considerations, electrical/electronic systems, basic engineering principles of ship stability and watertight integrity, the identification of hazardous materials, and emergency procedures. This supplement does not profess to make anyone an instant expert. It will, however, enable the novice to become familiar with the safety aspects of shipboard life in a very short time.

Accident Prevention and Safety at Sea - An Overview

Safety Philosophy

At sea, just as ashore, most accidents are preventable. However, the environment and working conditions aboard seagoing vessels pose additional hazards not found ashore. The responsibilities to avoid accidents flow from the top down; from the shore establishment to the Master, to each and every individual aboard. "Safety awareness" by all hands is the biggest single factor in reducing accidents.

As a researcher, you pride yourself in being knowledgeable and proficient in the demands of your discipline. You have undoubtedly acquired patience and a demand for attention to detail when working in the lab to ensure the validity of your research. The demand for such attributes is no less great when learning to live safely aboard a research vessel.

The old cliché "It's not my job" does not apply at sea. Ashore, you can go home and forget about work and the safety-related aspects of your work surroundings. You can easily travel a different route if there is construction work on your normal route. A power failure at home is an inconvenience. You are aware of any medical emergency only by the ambulance sirens. Aboard your ship, not only will you need to be aware of any construction or deck operations, you must be able to determine when and where it is safe to pass. A power failure aboard ship can be catastrophic. A medical emergency aboard ship affects everyone-you may be the only person available to assist the victim.

Accident-Causing Factors

As a research party member, you must learn to live and work safely in a potentially dangerous shipboard environment. Such factors as motion, noise, vibration, temperature extremes, close living conditions, rotating machinery, and lines under tension are not normally encountered on shore. Almost all who go to sea will, at one time or another, be seasick. The saying that you first fear that you will die and later fear that you won't is not too far from fact. A seasick person should be given only light duties until recovered and should never be assigned duties that require alertness, caution, or agility. Medicines that prevent motion sickness can sometimes cause drowsiness-beware of this! Ship's motion can cause fatigue in two ways. First, it's sometimes very difficult to sleep when the vessel is pitching and rolling. Even in fairly calm seas, it takes a newcomer one or two nights to adjust. Secondly, just moving about on a vessel in angry seas takes physical effort which in time, will wear down the most fit. Fatigue promotes carelessness.

When temperature extremes are too great, overall performance is impaired. Besides the debilitating effects of sunstroke, heat exhaustion, frostbite, hypothermia, etc., lesser physical impairments are possible. These include increased reaction time, decreased mental awareness, loss of dexterity and coordination, and fatigue.

Noise can have both a physiological and a psychological effect. Permanent hearing loss can be the result of sustained high noise level as well as extreme loud noises of short duration. Confinement aboard a ship in the fog can be unnerving with the constant sound of the fog horn hour after hour and even days on end. Similar detrimental effects can be caused by days of air gun firing. These noises create tension and an atmosphere which may promote an accident. Working around noisy equipment for an extended period of time can cause physical and psychological damage. It is important that you recognize and avoid these potential dangers.

The sun shines brightly at sea, causing glare conditions. Proper eye shading is a necessity. At the other end of the spectrum is night vision. A bright light on a dark bridge or other working area can be blinding. It takes several minutes readjusting your eyes. It is important that you determine the time needed to establish your night vision; it is equally important that you learn to avoid blinding others who have already established their night vision with an unmindful flashlight in the face or any bright white light, to a darkened condition-referred to as establishing *night vision*. Red lights do not have a blinding effect and must be used when maintaining night vision.

In a shipboard environment-especially confined spaces-you may be exposed to chemical agents in the air. Containing and exhausting laboratory fumes present an additional challenge aboard ships. Recognize these potential hazards! What is acceptable in a shoreside lab may not be suitable in a much more confined shipboard environment.

There are a number of factors which contribute to accidents; few accidents have a single cause. The immediate cause is usually the most apparent, but is not necessarily the underlying cause which may be harder to pinpoint and usually answers the question "why" for any accident. Some of the major factors contributing to accidents on research vessels are:

- Shipboard Environment
- Equipment and Materials
- Training and Experience
- Communications

At sea, slips and falls are the leading causes of injury. Do you know how to properly climb a ladder? Developing "sea legs" is not only gaining experience in navigating wet decks but also knowing what footwear to wear as well as learning to be wary and cautious.

If you do not want to go through life being called "Lefty," learn how to steady yourself without placing your hands on the doorjamb (the knife edge) when traveling through watertight doors.

Equipment and Material

Defective, improperly installed, or improperly used equipment is a major contributing cause of accidents. In doing research from a ship at sea, a lot of faith is placed in machinery and equipment. Whether deploying science packages, working in the labs, or going about your daily routine, you must rely on properly functioning shipboard and scientific equipment. The sudden failure of equipment due to overloading or defective materials almost always leads to an injury. Many pieces of machinery are inherently dangerous and are therefore provided with safety guards, warning signs, and are assigned safe working loads. Ignoring these safety features defeats their purpose.

What are the side effects of some motion sickness medicines? What are the more subtle physical impairments of temperature extremes? Do you know why ships use internal red light at night? Do you know how the basic deck machinery works and where not to be when it is activated? Do you know how or even why you would want to dog a hatch? Learning to find your way around the ship, to understand the terminology, and to recognize factors that have traditionally proven to be causes of accidents takes a little time; take time now!

Training and Experience

A lack of skill, experience, and knowledge concerning shipboard procedures can easily lead to accidents. During your initial exposure to a procedure or a piece of equipment, extra care and supervision may be necessary until everyone is far enough along on the "learning curve" to make for a safe operation. By paying attention and learning proper procedures, you can eliminate unnecessary accidents.

Communications

People react to what they think they hear, not necessarily what the person speaking actually says. Poor communications due to such factors as language barriers, unfamiliar terminology, background noise, or failure to speak distinctly lead to misunderstanding, mistakes, and ultimately, accidents. The person in charge must establish and maintain good communications in order to coordinate the efforts of a team. Listen so that you clearly understand the hazards you face and their possible consequences.

Accident Prevention

An effective accident prevention program is built on the tenets of management and supervisory commitment, safety awareness, and training.

Management and Supervisory Commitment

This includes budgeting time and funds for safety-related activities and equipment; the willingness to reject unsafe practices which might at times, especially under pressure, seem expedient; and positive reaction when risks and/or safer ways to do things are pointed out by crew members.

Shipboard living aboard a research vessel is not a passive exercise-if you are not constantly aware of your surroundings, then you can endanger yourself and other crew and scientific members. Although your circumstances as a research party member may not allow you to participate in most shipboard duties, the limited amenities and services of a research vessel require that at the very least you be able to take care of yourself.

Safety Awareness

Safety aspects of every operation should be routinely considered by all hands. All hands should be aware of the effectiveness of the safety program. The RVOC has collected accident statistics showing the collective accident rate to be rather low (good). However, there is no justification for accepting the current rate as "good enough" since virtually all accidents can be prevented.

Learning to move around your vessel will provide you many new challenges. When climbing vertical ladders, always face the ladder-do not attempt to go backwards. Always hold on to the rail. Avoid using portable ladders unless absolutely necessary-and then, only if it is lashed to an immovable object.

When two or more people are using the ladder at the same time, the second person should stay far enough below as not to get kicked in the head, and should not look upward in case of falling dirt or rust. Avoid carrying large objects up or down ladders or stairs; instead, pass or hoist them in assembly-line fashion. Avoid blocking stairwells while stopped in conversation or by placing an object in front of stairs or ladders.

Corridors and passageways should be kept free. While entrance and exit passageways serve as travel routes from one end of the ship to another, they also serve as emergency exit routes. Never block entrance and exit passages with objects. When objects are stored in a passageway, they should not block or be on top of any emergency escape hatch.

Watertight doors normally remain closed, even during calm seas. Watertight doors that are required to be open are done so by latching them in an open position (even in calm seas, be very wary of watertight doors that "swing" with the ship). During heavy weather, dog all watertight doors. Dog the side opposite the hinge side first.

Training

Ships' crews and researchers must be trained in both emergency procedures and in safe practices. The RVOC Safety Training Manual is to be the basis for such training.

Orientation

Introduction

Immediately prior to or immediately after departure, the research party and new crew members, upon hearing the general alarm, gather at a central location with their life jackets. At this time, you will receive an orientation for new people regarding shipboard safety.

The following are normally included in an orientation for new people regarding shipboard safety:

- An explanation of the general alarm signals and where and how personnel should proceed to assigned stations.

- An explanation of station bill and bunk cards.
- How to don life jackets and survival suits.
- What to do in case of man overboard, fire, and other emergencies.
- Requirements for hard hats, shoes, exposure suits, work vests, harnesses, and safety lines.
- When, how, and who to notify for over-the-side research.
- Discussion of other matters of general safety interest.
- Shipboard drills.

Station Bill

A vessel's Station Bill assigns each person aboard various duties associated with emergencies. It also assigns individuals to muster stations and survival craft. On many research vessels, the Station Bill is specifically for vessel crew members, while a subset of the Station Bill as well as emergency procedure information (also referred to as a *Bunk Card*) is posted in research party staterooms. Everyone is given an orientation of the vessel and instructions. Part of your orientation is to ensure that you know your assigned stations and duties as listed on the Station Bill, and if applicable, your *Bunk Card*. Examine these documents carefully; memorize your duties and muster station. You should know two routes for getting out of your living and working spaces in the event of emergency situations.

The Station Bill lists the various *emergency signals* to be used for calling the crew and the research party members to their stations or to give instructions while at their stations. Your vessel uses standard signals, commonly used in the merchant fleet and required to regulatory agencies. The Master of your vessel may establish additional emergency signals that ensure that all crew members and research party members take positive notice of the

Fire Stations or Fire Drills

The fire alarm signal is a continuous blast of the whistle for a period of not less than 10 seconds, supplemented by the continuous ringing of the general alarm bells for not less than 10 seconds.

For dismissal from fire stations, there are three short blasts of the whistle and three short rings on the general alarm.

Boat Stations or Boat Drills

The signal for boat stations or drill is a succession of more than six short blasts followed by one long blast of the whistle supplemented by a comparable signal on the general alarm bells.

Where whistle signals are used for handling the lifeboats, they are as follows:

- To lower lifeboats, one short blast.
- To stop lowering the lifeboats, two short blasts.

For dismissal from boat stations, there are three short blasts of the whistle and three short rings on the general alarm.

GENERAL SAFETY PRECAUTIONS

Many injuries and accidents can be avoided by using the proper tools and following safety precautions. The extra ten minutes saved by not following procedures may result in a long-term injury. Most general safety precautions are normally routine practices that we often neglect when we are in a hurry.

Most staterooms and corridors have smoke detectors similar to those used in homes. Learn what to do and where to go when you hear its shrill alarm.

The following are a few examples of common shipboard safety practices:

- When sea conditions are rough and topside work is being performed, everyone works in pairs. You should always wear a work vest.
- Because lines, deck openings, or wet surfaces can cause falls and slips, one eye should always be kept on the deck while walking.

- Bare feet are allowed only in staterooms.
- Examine all labels and warnings before using any equipment or products. If there is a question as to the use of a tool, product, or piece of machinery, consult the proper authority before proceeding.
- Always know the function of anything before touching it.
- Wipe up any spill immediately-the decks are slippery enough!

Seamanship/Deck and Science Operations

Small Boats

All personnel embarked in small boats should have a basic knowledge of seamanship. They should be aware of the particular dangers associated with small boats, stability of the boat and safety of all personnel being considered foremost. When you board a small boat prior to removal of the hoisting equipment, you must wear a hard hat. Wear a lifejacket when boarding or debarking. The boat should not be hoisted until all personnel have debarked.

- Your conduct aboard a boat should emphasize safety.
- Become familiar with basic emergency radio procedures.
- Learn the emergency response procedures prior to any voyage.

When transferring from a small boat to the research vessel, time your "jump" to the boarding ladder. Make the jump at the time you are able to reach the highest point on the boarding ladder. Keep your hands inboard to avoid crushing them between the boat and ship's side.

Loading and Stowage

A ship's officer is responsible for loading, handling, and stowage of cargo and scientific gear; the Chief Mate is responsible for securing deck areas, the Chief Engineer for engineering spaces, and the Chief Steward for commissary, galley, and dining spaces. The Chief Scientist is responsible for securing gear and equipment in science laboratories and storage areas; however, since some researchers may not be experienced mariners, the work is checked by the Chief Mate and the marine technicians prior to getting underway. On research ships, gear is loaded either by hand or cranes. Before heavy lifts are made with shipboard cranes, the Master is informed so that steps can be taken if necessary to ensure adequate stability for the operation. The Master is also consulted for the placement of heavy items such as winches and vans.

Since storm tracks are far from predictable, everyone should be prepared for the worst. The ship should be battened down. Battening down includes securing heavy topside pieces of science equipment with wire or chain; checking all spaces for loose gear; dogging down weather doors, hatches, and vents; and general increasing watertight integrity.

Prior to encountering heavy weather, the ship is *battened down* to ensure the vessel's watertight integrity. Lifelines are rigged, "no-go" areas designated, and a system implemented to account for personnel who must go out on weather decks. You will need to secure gear in your stateroom and work area.

Deck Operations

Deck machinery and deck systems are used to move cargo, handle mooring lines and anchors, and launch and recover scientific apparatus and boats to support the missions of oceanographic research vessels. The inherent hazards of working near tensioned cables, rotating machinery, and heavy moving weights are increased when these operations are conducted on the heaving deck of a vessel at sea. Individuals can be injured by cables or machinery, knocked overboard (possibly unconscious), or injured by flying debris if safety precautions are not followed.

Extreme care must be exercised when working in the vicinity of frames to ensure that personnel are not knocked overboard or pinned between the frame and other structures when rigging the frame in or out.

Snapback results from the energy stored in a line as it is stretched. If a tensioned line parts or is released suddenly, the line "snaps back" to its original length-much like an elastic band. You should stay well clear of potential recoil paths of any line or cable in use.

The following safety precautions should be observed during all deck operations:

- Observe all posted safety precautions.
- Keep clear of loaded lines, wires, and cables.
- Avoid getting hands, feet, or loose clothing caught in bights of line, wire, or cables, or in rotating machinery such as moving frames.
- Keep loose gear away from open cargo hatches. Personnel below could be injured by falling objects.
- Keep noise to a minimum-confusion and misunderstanding between operators and workers can lead to serious injury and damage to equipment.
- Do not permit horseplay.
- If you are not a member of the deck operation crew, keep clear of deck operations.

General safety precautions for weight handling equipment:

- Stay clear of moving equipment such as cranes, frames, booms, and davits.
- Wear adequate foot protection.
- Wear hard hats.

General Safety Precautions

In addition to the safety considerations for each individual system, the following general safety precautions should be observed at all times while in the vicinity of operating specialized oceanographic deck systems:

- Keep clear of the wire or cable on deck leading over the side. The weight of the wire or cable, plus the weight of the package, result in high tension which creates a potential personal hazard should the cable part.

- The abrupt movement of the cable or rigging in and out of frames can cause serious injury to unsuspecting personnel.

Leather gloves should be worn when handling wire rope, except when it is moving. Gloves, if snagged, can drag the wearer into danger.

Science Operations

Much of research ship time is spent performing science operations, which include towing instruments, working gear over the side or fantail, or placing heavy objects on the seafloor. On a large ship, there may be many independent groups working on different projects at the same time. Nothing goes over the side unless permission from the watch officer is obtained-whether launching scientific gear or disposing garbage.

When scientific gear goes under the ship, it could entangle the ship's rudder or propeller. This can be extremely dangerous when line or cable is going over the side. As it becomes wound up in the propeller, line and the attached equipment may whip off the deck, injuring persons in the process. If during launching or pickup of towed gear, it appears the propeller or rudder may be fouled, the watch officer will immediately stop the screw.

When working over the side, observe proper safety precautions at all times. Wear a safety harness; a lifejacket or work vest must be worn over the safety harness. Double-check all knots. This should be done by another crew member who is fully qualified in marlinespike seamanship. Watch out for the "Might Knot"-the knot that might NOT hold!

Possible towing hazards include:

- Entangling gear in the rudder or screw.
- Engaging gear with other gear off the same vessel, a nearby vessel, or a mooring.

- Becoming "hung-up." When the science gear breaks loose, locked-in potential energy in the towline becomes kinetic energy. People in the path of the towline can be hurt. Stay clear of a towline when it is hung up; nonessential personnel should leave open decks.

Health and Medical

Personal Care

Proper diet, rest, hygiene, and attitude are all contributing factors to maintaining a healthy body-both physically and mentally. When you are not in the proper physical or mental state, your actions may adversely affect the well-being of other personnel.

Attitude When on board a ship, adjust your attitudes to adapt to tight working and living quarters and many different types of personalities. Cigarette smoke is irritating to many people. It is important to be considerate when others are asleep; noise level should be kept down to a minimum at all times.

Due to the close quarters of shipboard living, a clean body and clothing are a must.

Rest The ability to function properly and to maintain the body's resistance to disease and infections depends on adequate rest. When fatigue sets in, strength, coordination, judgment, and attitude are adversely affected. If you feel fatigue setting in, inform your supervisor; failing to do so could put the ship and crew in jeopardy.

Diet A proper diet is necessary to maintain the body's energy level. Without proper eating habits, fatigue sets in at a quickened pace and resistance to diseases, colds, and infections is lowered. While at sea, the sun and salt air deplete the body's fluid and salt levels. To compensate for this loss, increase your intake of liquids and salt. If you are on a special diet due to a medical reason (diabetes, high cholesterol, etc.), report this information well in advance of the cruise so that meals and provisions can be properly planned.

Personal Hygiene Personal hygiene is important. It makes a statement to others about your attitude. An unclean body fosters unpleasant odors and a greater chance of the development of skin ailments and/or diseases, especially in humid and cramped quarters.

Drugs and Alcohol The use of drugs and/or alcohol does affect the way you perform. Emergencies are usually unannounced and unexpected; a functionally impaired individual would be more of a hindrance than a help. When an individual is drunk or impaired, there is an increased chance of falling overboard, falling off a ladder, slipping on a wet deck, etc. Many prescription and nonprescription medicines (antihistamines, cough syrups, etc.) have side effects that can impair judgment and the ability to function properly. If taking medication, you should consult a physician or pharmacist to find a medication that alleviates the problem while causing the least amount of side effects. If you are required by a physician to take prescription medication, notify your supervisor; bring an adequate supply of the medication for the duration of the cruise.

All UNOLS vessels have a policy of "Zero Tolerance" towards illegal drugs and support Federal regulations concerning the use of alcohol.

Proper Clothing Bring appropriate clothing. Sunblock and clothing that provide protection against the sun are recommended when traveling to warm climates. Colder climates, naturally, require warmer clothing. Wool and polypropylene materials provide warmth and repel moisture. These materials also retain their insulating properties when wet. In either climate, proper head covering is necessary. Footwear should fit properly. Tired or sore feet can cause considerable problems such as backache and general discomfort. Shoes should have nonslip soles, and steel toes are recommended for deck operations, cargo handling, or other heavy jobs. Foul weather gear should include a jacket, pants, head covering, and proper footwear. Because ship space is limited, the amount of clothing, as well as the type, should be considered when planning a cruise. Bring enough underclothing to last ten days without laundry facilities. Sandals are not permitted when working on a wet deck, near machinery, or in a laboratory.

Chapter 15

Ship Sanitation

Ship sanitation is critical to the health and attitude of personnel as well as the smooth operation of a ship. The careless disposal of materials not only posses a safety hazard but also detracts from the appearance of the ship. Personnel should clean up work areas; dispose of trash in the proper containers; and wash down the work surface when work is complete. Mops should be rinsed in hot soapy water and left out to dry before stowing-this prevents odors and germs from forming. Liquid spills and/or broken objects should be cleaned up at once. It is imperative to inform the Master immediately if a container of hazardous material breaks or spills. The spillage could cause damage to the ship or injury to the crew. Personnel living spaces serve as home for the duration of the cruise. Shared living quarters must be kept neat as a courtesy to fellow members. Dirty laundry may cause offensive odors and should be put away; bed linen should be changed at least once a week. Toilet/shower facilities must be kept clean and drains unclogged.

MEDICAL

When medical problems occur at sea, more attention is needed than when in port because of the distance from qualified medical personnel. Small problems, left unattended, can become major emergencies.

General Precruise Medical Requirements

All personnel should have a complete physical as required by their institution. A dental exam is also highly recommended. The above may seem like a waste of time and money, but it should be remembered that as the vessel undergoes an overhaul periodically, so should you. All appropriate inoculations (including tetanus) that are necessary for ports of call should be up-to-date. If you need inoculations-whether daily or in an emergency (for diabetes or allergic reactions)-ensure that another person knows how to administer the medication. General medical information should be provided by each person on board. This should include any past or current medical problems (such as diabetes, high blood pressure, etc.), inoculation record, allergy information, prescription drug usage and dosage, and generic names for prescription drugs. Eye prescriptions should be listed for personnel who wear eyeglasses, and an extra pair of eyeglasses should be carried on board.

If during orientation you somehow missed being introduced to the crew member who acts as the vessel's corpsman (normally one of the Mates), find out now *who he or she is* and the location of the dispensary.

General Information

The names of personnel who are qualified to administer general first aid, CPR, or emergency medical treatment are posted. At the beginning of the cruise, you will be informed of the location of emergency equipment (eyewash stations, wash-down showers, fresh water, emergency oxygen, etc.) and how to use it.

First Aid Kits

First aid kits are located throughout the vessel and are equipped with basic medical supplies, including Band-Aids, eyewash solutions, ointments, etc.

Seasickness

Medications may be carried on board and dispensed as needed for seasickness. If you get seasick, drink plenty of fluids to prevent dehydration.

Sunburn

Sunburn can be very painful and bothersome and may occur quickly. It only takes about four hours to get second-degree burns in the Tropics. In the case of mild sunburn, moisturizing creams such as Aloe Vera should be applied. The affected area should be covered to avoid further exposure to the sun. Also, drink plenty of fluids to avoid dehydration. Exposure time to direct sun should be increased gradually. Clean the burn area and apply cold water to relieve pain of severe sunburn. The best way you can avoid sunburn is to use a sunblock, wear protective clothing, and limit exposure time to direct sunlight.

First Aid

Proper administration of first aid can mean the difference between life and death, short-long-term recovery, and permanent or temporary disability. First aid is an interim step until professional medical treatment can be sought. There are two steeps that should occur as quickly as possible in a medical emergency: first, ensuring the victim's immediate survival, secondly, summoning assistance. Before going to sea, all personnel should have a basic knowledge of the more serious medical emergencies that can develop and the first steps in treatment.

When approaching an accident victim, survey the area before entering. There may still be danger (i.e., live electrical lines, rotating machinery, hazardous materials, lack of oxygen, etc.)

Hypothermia

The condition of hypothermia results when body temperature is reduced because of exposure to cold water or air. While at sea, it is important to remember that exposure to cold water causes heat loss twenty times faster than exposure to cold air. Even a few minutes of exposure under these conditions can cause hypothermia. Hypothermia can even take place in tropical waters. A victim of hypothermia should be treated at once. The first step is to get the victim to a warm area. Secondly, all cold, wet clothing should be removed and the extremities wrapped in blankets.

The torso area should be covered and a hat should be placed on the victim's head. The first area to warm up is the torso, since this area contains all the vital organs of the body. A good way for the rescuer to warm this area is to remove his or her clothing (shirt) and jump around for a few minutes to elevate the body temperature then lie down chest to chest with the victim. This method transfers the heat of one body to another. A warm or hot shower should never be used to warm a victim of hypothermia. The circulatory system to the extremities has been shut down by the body to keep the warm blood near the vital organs. A warm or hot shower would make the body resume full blood circulation throughout the body before the blood in the extremities is warm enough. The shock of the cold blood from the extremities to the vital organs could be more than the body could withstand. Shivering is a good sign because it means the body's natural defense mechanism is working. The body or limbs of a hypothermia victim should not be rubbed due to the possibility of more damage occurring to a circulatory system that is already in severe shock.

Even if a hypothermia victim is not breathing when found, treatment must be initiated at once. It's the body's natural defense mechanism to shut down as much as possible.

LIFESAVING EQUIPMENT AND SURVIVAL PROCEDURES

Introduction

The sea can be a fierce, unforgiving force of nature, capable of sending a ship to the bottom, and its crew "into the drink." Without the proper equipment to protect you from the weather, provide sustenance, signal rescue resources, and, above all, keep you afloat, the odds are heavily against your ability to survive. The only defense you have is the proper amount and type of lifesaving equipment, ready for immediate use. This equipment is vital to survival. Survival at sea depends on sufficient and properly maintained lifesaving equipment coupled with training in survival procedures and the proper use of the equipment.

Pimary Lifesaving Equipment

Primary Lifesaving Equipment means "a lifeboat or an acceptable substitute." The acceptable substitutes include inflatable life rafts, rescue boats, and, under certain conditions, buoyant apparatus and life floats. However the vessel is equipped, these lifesaving appliances are the first line of defense.

Lifeboats

Research vessels carry sufficient numbers of lifeboats or life rafts to accommodate 100% of the persons on board. Boat drills are conducted weekly.

Inflatable Life Rafts

Inflatable life rafts are the primary lifesaving equipment on most research vessels. They are mounted as far outboard as possible, free of overhead obstructions, and high enough to be protected from heavy seas. A hydrostatic release and *weak link* are provided on each container to allow for automatic deployment and inflation of the raft should the vessel sink before the rafts can be deployed. Rafts may be removed from cradles and moved to opposite sides and launched by hand if necessary. Instruction cards for the proper stowage and launching of inflatable life rafts are posted in various locations throughout the ship.

Buoyant Apparatus

A buoyant apparatus is a flat, box-like flotation device with grab lines installed around its edges; the life float is similar to the buoyant apparatus except it is open in the center and fitted with a net and wooden floor suspended from the center of the float. Buoyant apparatus and life floats are stowed on an open deck or in racks in such a manner to be *float-free* in case of emergency.

Rescue Boat

The handling of oceanographic equipment creates a potential risk for falling overboard. Since a ship with equipment over the side is usually unable to maneuver freely for a recovery, the *rescue boat* provides a rapid means of rescuing the victim. It is also ideal for marshaling all the ship's inflatable life rafts or buoyant apparatus in the event the ship has sunk and motor lifeboats are not available. A rescue boat is generally a small, lightweight boat of rigid or semirigid construction fitted with built-in buoyancy and an outboard motor.

Secondary Lifesaving Equipment

While primary lifesaving equipment is provided for the entire crew and is designed for extended survival, *Secondary Lifesaving Equipment* is provided for individual survival in distress situations. These items will allow a person to remain afloat until rescued.

Lifejackets

All vessels are required to carry one Type 1 Adult *Lifejacket* for every person on board. A Type 1 jacket is designed to turn a person face up in the water. Additional lifejackets are accessible to the engine room, bridge, and science labs in sufficient numbers to accommodate all persons normally on watch or working in these areas.

Ring Lifebuoys

Ring Lifebuoys are the first means of rescue for the person who falls overboard. Lightweight and round, the ring buoy is easy to toss to the victim and will keep him or her afloat until help can arrive.

Lifejackets are distributed throughout the crew's and scientists' quarters, providing one lifejacket per bunk, and stowed so that they are readily accessible.

All lifejackets are provided with a light, whistle, and retroflective tape.

Immersion (Exposure) Suits

Prolonged exposure to the elements of the sea, especially in cold waters, presents many challenges to an individual's survival, not the least of which is hypothermia-the rapid and continued loss of body heat. *Immersion Suits* are designed to provide full-body thermal protection similar to a diver's wet suit, as well as built-in flotation, and are required to be on vessels operating in higher latitudes.

Work Vests Precautions should be taken to avoid unnecessary lifesaving situations. A work vest may be used by persons working on deck or in small boats where the bulk of a regular Type 1 lifejacket would be confining. The work vest is not a substitute for a lifejacket!

When working near or over the water during science operations, a work vest may be the deciding factor in your survival.

Thermal Protective Aids

The *Thermal Protective Aid (TPA)* is a multi-purpose item of lifesaving equipment. The TPA is a bag or suit made of waterproof material with low thermal conductivity. Its function is to minimize the effects of hypothermia or aid in the recovery of a hypothermia victim. It may be used as an alternative for immersion suits while in a life raft or lifeboat, or a person suffering from hypothermia may be placed inside so that body heat is maintained inside the bag.

General Lifesaving Equipment and Inforation

Not all casualties at sea result in "taking to lifeboats." Distress situations are more often limited to vessel breakdowns, personnel evacuations, or other instances which require that the vessel be located and assisted by a search and rescue resource. To facilitate the rescue efforts, research vessels carry various devices for location and signaling.

Distress Signals

When a mariner sees a flare displayed in the night sky or unusual smoke rising from the horizon, the first thought is that of a vessel in distress. Not only do these displays indicate a distress, but they mark the location of the vessel. For this reason, *distress signals* are a necessary part of a ship's lifesaving equipment. The *RVSS* manual requires *all* research vessels to carry at least 12 red rocket flares. Research vessels also carry additional visual signals, such as searchlights, international code flags, and signaling lights.

Line-Throwing Appliance

In situations where a line must be passed over some distance, the *line-throwing appliance* may save considerable time and effort while providing a greater margin of safety than the conventional heaving line. A line-throwing appliance may be considered when attempting to pass a line to a person overboard. In such cases, only the lightweight, plastic-tipped form of projectile should be employed.

Epirb

The *Emergency Position Indicating Radio Beacon (EPIRB)* is a battery-operated, self-activating emergency transmitter. The unit is stowed in a rack, inverted, with the power switch in *automatic*. When righted, the EPIRB sends out a radio signal to search and rescue resources. An aircraft or vessel can *home in* on the signal and follow it to a disabled vessel's exact location.

Survival Procedures

Having to abandon ship is a traumatic experience-gone are the comforts and security of the vessel. Exposed to the elements, either in lifeboats or rafts, or immersed in the water with only a lifejacket, survival at sea in a distress situation depends on an individual's knowledge and training in survival procedures. This is NOT a hopeless situation. Modern technology now makes distress communications and location by rescue resources a *routine* operation.

General

The Station Bill is where preparations for distress situations begin. It is here that the crew is assigned various duties associated with emergencies (including what equipment to bring, such as an EPIRB) and individuals are assigned to muster stations and survival craft.

Abandon Ship

When the time arrives for the ultimate in survival procedure, having to Abandon Ship, conduct the evolution in a calm, orderly manner-without panic! With adequate preparations and training, there should be no difficulty in carrying out a safe evacuation.

Training

Being properly prepared is the best way to ensure survival at sea. Since it is somewhat impractical to actually sink a ship for practice, the alternative is *training*. Crew members and research personnel should be thoroughly trained in all aspects of survival techniques from the Station Bill to launching lifeboats. You should participate in the weekly emergency drills as if they were the real thing. Report to stations fully clothed, wear shoes, put on your lifejacket, and bring your immersion suit. In an actual emergency, you may not have time to go back to your quarters.

When the command "Prepare to Abandon Ship" is passed, along with the appropriate emergency signal, the crew instantly begins a planned series of actions similar to the following scenario:

- Muster at your assigned station; provide all equipment to the scene as assigned on the Station Bill; come to your station fully clothed with your lifejacket on and carrying your immersion suit. If there is sufficient time before the actual evolution begins, don your immersion suit first and keep your lifejacket handy. The suit provides flotation and protects you from the elements.
- *Prepare* all survival craft for immediate launching. Swing out lifeboats or prepare life rafts according to standard procedures. DO not laugh any equipment

until instructed to do so by the Master. Stand by calmly at your station and await further orders.

- When the Master orders "Abandon Ship," launch all survival craft. Enter boats and rafts using ladders rather than jumping over the side. Keep calm and organized.
- Once boarded, all rafts or boats are tethered and towed away from the ship by a motor lifeboat or the rescue boat. Keep all craft together in the vicinity of the ship's last position.
- While waiting for rescue units to arrive, maintain a continuous visual and radio communication watch. Your lifeboat or life raft is well-stocked with equipment and provisions to sustain life *comfortably*. Use the supplies in the survival craft with care-they may have to last a while. Just sit back, relax, and await rescue.

FIRE PREVENTION AND CONTROL

Introduction

Fire prevention should be part of everyday shipboard routine. Because accidents do happen, the ability to control and extinguish a fire quickly is essential to the safety of the vessel and everyone aboard. Persons aboard a research vessel are particularly at risk because their vessel often operates independently in remote areas and is at sea for long, extended periods. Should a fire occur, they must be self-sufficient, since the nearest assistance from shore or another vessel may well be hundreds of miles and several days away. Therefore knowledge, training, and experience with regard to fire safety are imperative to the UNOLS fleet.

Keep Combustibles and Hazardous Materials off the Ship

"If it isn't there, it won't burn"-this philosophy applies to materials brought aboard ship as well as those used in its construction.

There are some basic principles of ship design that can reduce the risk of fire. To prevent fire from spreading, UNOLS vessels are divided into zones that usually coincide with subdivision watertight bulkheads. Main vertical zone boundaries consist of insulated steel bulkheads designed to contain fire, smoke, and heat within limits. Spaces in which fire is most likely to occur, such as laboratories, galleys, and machinery spaces, are required to be separated by similar boundaries. Many materials used in the construction of research vessels are noncumbustible. Some UNOLS vessels have permanently installed detection systems that sound an alarm in a normally manned space such as the pilothouse. These devices are similar to smoke alarms found in modern homes. Doors are fitted on all spaces, and ventilation systems are segregated by fire zones to assist in containing any fire. Spaces having greatest fire risk have a fixed extinguishing system. Ships are designed so that two fire hoses will reach any part of the vessel. Two means of escape are provided from every space that is normally occupied. If one access is blocked by fire, another is always available.

Smoking can be particularly hazardous aboard ship. An improperly disposed cigarette or cigar butt can ignite other materials. Smoking is prohibited in certain areas and under certain conditions, such as while in your bunk, while the ship is refueling, or while in ship spaces such as paint lockers, battery rooms, and laboratories. Cigarette butts must be disposed of safely-preferably by drowning in water, or snubbing out in ashtrays or other proper containers.

Many fires have been started by bunk lights. Light bulbs generate a great deal of heat and under certain conditions can cause surrounding materials to catch fire. Fires have been started from bedding placed over the top of bunk lights.

Classification of Fire

Fires are classified by the National Fire Protection Association (NFPA). Fire classification is used to select the proper type of fire extinguisher. There are four basic fire classifications, lettered A, B, C, and D.

Class A fires are those fueled by combustible solids such as wood, paper, clothing, bedding, and some plastics; any material which leaves an ash. These fires can be extinguished by the use of water.

Class B fires involve flammable or combustible liquids, flammable gases, greases, and similar products. These fires can best be extinguished by smothering agents, such as foam, CO2, and dry chemicals. Water spray can also be used.

Class C fires are fueled by energized electrical equipment, conductors, or appliances. To protect personnel from shock, nonconducting extinguishing agents, such as CO2, Halon, or dry chemical must be used. Secure electrical power to the circuit causing the problem.

Class D fires involve combustible metals, e.g., sodium, potassium, magnesium, titanium, and aluminum. These fires are extinguished through the use of a heat-absorbing extinguishing agent, such as certain dry powders (different from dry chemicals), that do not react with the burning metals. Specific firefighting agents are used for specific metals.

Knowing the classifications of fire and what type of extinguisher to use on each type of fire is not enough information to fight a fire effectively. You should know where extinguishers are, how to activate them, where to aim the agent, how much to use, how and when to notify others.

Firefighting Equipment

Portable Fire Extinguishers Portable extinguishers are used for a fast attack that will knock down flames. They can be carried to the fire. However, since they are small, continuous application can be sustained for only a minute or less. Portable extinguishers are classed with one or more letters and with a numeral. The letters correspond to the class/classes of fire on which the extinguisher is effective. A Class A extinguisher should be used on a wood or bedding fire, while a Class C extinguisher should be used on an electrical fire. A Class AB extinguisher should be used on fires involving common combustibles, such as wood, and also on fuel oil, or both. The

NFPA rates portable extinguishers with Arabic numerals according to their efficiency. An extinguisher rated 4A extinguishes twice as much Class A fire as a 2A extinguisher, etc. The Coast Guard uses Roman numerals to indicate the sizes of portable extinguishers, with I being the smallest size and V being the largest size.

Safety Rules for Portable Extinguishers

If you discover a fire, call out the discovery, sound the fire alarm, and summon help. Close door to isolate the fire if it can be done quickly and safely.

- Never pass a fire to get to an extinguisher. A dead-end passageway can trap you.
- If you must enter a room or compartment, don't let the fire get between you and the door.
- If you enter a room or compartment and your attack with a portable extinguisher fails, get out immediately. Close the door to confine the fire and wait for the help you called. Your knowledge will help them.

Water Extinguishers Water extinguishers use water or a water solution as the extinguishing agent. In general, water extinguishers have application for only Class A fires, except for the foam-type extinguishers which may be used on Class A and B fires. These extinguishers hold 2½ gallons of liquid and discharge their contents in less than a minute. The stored-pressure extinguisher is activated by first pulling the ring pin. The hose is then directed with one hand while the discharge lever is squeezed with the other hand. The stream is aimed at the base of the fire and moved back and forth for complete coverage. Short bursts can be used to conserve water.

Carbon Dioxide Extinguishers. Portable carbon dioxide extinguishers are used primarily for Class B and C fires, with the most common sizes having 5 to 20 pounds of CO2. These extinguishers have a range of about 3 to 8 feet and will discharge their contents in 30 seconds or less. A CO2 extinguisher is activated by removing the locking pin and squeezing two handles together while holding the hose handle (not the horn) in the other hand. For combating a Class B fire, the horn should be aimed at the base of the fire nearest the operator and then "swept" slowly back and forth across the fire. To combat a Class C fire, the electrical equipment should be de-energized and the horn discharge aimed at the base of the fire. It is important that the hose handle be held and not the horn so that ice or frost that forms on the horn cannot become a current path to the operator if the horn should come in contact with live electrical parts.

Dry Chemical Extinguishers Dry chemical portable extinguishers, available in several different sizes, use any one of five different dry chemical agents as an extinguishing medium. These extinguishers have at least a BC rating, while some have an ABC rating. Portable cartridge-operated extinguishers range in size from 2 to 30 pounds, while semiportable models contain up to 50 pounds of extinguishing agent. Units under 10 pound have a discharge duration of 8-10 seconds; the larger units have up to 30 seconds of discharge time. The cartridge-operated extinguisher uses a small cartridge filled with inert gas mounted on the side of the cylinder to propel the extinguishing agent. The extinguisher is activated by removing the ring pin, and depressing the puncturing pin. These actions release the propellant gas which forces the extinguishing agent up to the nozzle. The discharge should be directed at the seat of the fire, starting at the near edge. The stream should be moved from side to side with rapid motions, to sweep the fire off the fuel. The initial discharge should not be directed onto the burning material at close range (3 to 8 feet), as the stream of extinguishing agent may scatter the fire or spray burning liquid about. The agent may be applied in short bursts by opening and closing the nozzle with the squeeze grips.

When activating a cartridge-operated dry chemical extinguisher, aim the top of the cylinder away from you. If the top has not been screwed on properly, it may come off violently and cause injury when the propellant gas charges the cylinder. Also, test the extinguisher before taking it into a fire by giving the hose nozzle a quick squeeze-then you know whether it will work or not.

Halon Extinguishers Halon portable fire extinguishers come in two types, Halon 1211 and Halon 1301, and several sizes from 1 to 20 pounds. They are rated for Class B and C fires. Some Halon 1211 extinguishers are also rated for use on Class A fires. The discharge range from these extinguishers is from 4 to 15 feet and they are discharged quickly. Halon 1211 is not affected by the wind as much as CO_2 or Halon 1301 and on a weight-of-agent basis is at least twice as effective as CO_2. Persons should avoid breathing the extinguishing agent or the gases produced by the thermal decomposition. Halon 1301 is at least as effective as ---on a weight-of-agent basis, is suitable for cold weather operation, and leaves no residue. On Class B fires, Halon from portable extinguishers is applied in the same manner as CO_2.

Semiportable Fire Extinguishers A semiportable fire extinguisher (or extinguishing system) is one from which a hose can be run out to the fire. The two types of semiportable systems are: CO_2 hose-reel and dry chemical hose systems. Semiportable fire extinguishers provide a means of getting a sizable amount of extinguishing agent to a fire rapidly. These systems have greater capacity and have slightly more range (nozzle to fire distance) than hand-portable extinguishers. As the name implies, they are only semiportable and fires may be fought only within the range allowed by the discharge hose. They cannot be carried about the ship like hand-portable extinguishers.

Fixed Fire Extinguishing Systems Fixed fire extinguishing systems are usually built into the ship at the time of its construction. These systems are carefully designed: they consider the fire risks aboard the vessel, must meet exacting regulatory standards, and are available for use in an emergency. If a large fire develops, such as one in a machinery space, these systems may be the best means to extinguish it. There are four types of fixed systems common to UNOLS vessels: the fire main system, carbon dioxide system, Halon 1301 system, and the galley range system.

If you do fight the fire, remember the word: PASS

PULL the pin.....Some extinguishers require releasing a lock latch, pressing a puncture lever, or other motion.

AIM low.....pointing the extinguisher nozzle (or its horn or hose) at the base of the fire.

SQUEEZE the handle.....This releases the extinguishing agent.

SWEEP from side to side.....at the base of the fire until it appears to be out. Watch the fire area. If fire breaks out again, repeat use of the extinguisher.

Most portable extinguishers work according to these directions, but some do not. Read and follow the directions on your extinguisher-on each one if you have more than one make or model.

Protect yourself at all times! Stay low. Avoid breathing the heated smoke and fumes or the extinguishing agent.

If the fire starts to spread or threatens your escape route, get out immediately.

Combating the Fire

When a fire is noticed, the first thing to do is sound an alarm. The pilothouse must be notified of the location, and if known, the type of fire. This is important no matter how small the fire. It can be done by intercom, sound-powered phone, going to or sending someone else to the pilothouse, or by yelling.

Don't be a hero and try to fight a fire without sounding an alarm first. A fire can quickly get out of control and you could be trapped or overcome.

If the fire is small, the previous information is designed to help you choose the right extinguisher and put it out. If the fire is larger or gets out of control, then the training, coordination, efficient use of manpower, and a more thorough assessment of the situation that comes with the crew's damage control team will be necessary.

If your first indication of a possible fire is the sight or smell of smoke coming from a closed compartment, you must be careful before opening that space. Feel the door or hatch for heat (cautiously, with the back of your hand). If it is hot or warm, do not open it. Notify the pilothouse or firefighting party immediately.

Stability and Watertight Integrity

Stability

Stability of a ship depends on the hull form chosen by the designer and how the weights, such as fuel, stores, provisions, scientific equipment, etc., are distributed about the ship. Vessel operators have little control over the vessel's form. They do, however, have great control over how much weight is taken aboard, how and where that weight is stowed, and the consequent effects on vessel stability.

As a research party member, you have the responsibility of making known to the crew the nature and amount of weights you have brought on board, and strictly abide by the Master's instructions regarding weight stowage and locations, particularly liquid weights and weights stowed high in the ship. Because all stability assessments assume a watertight shell and weather deck, everyone must keep watertight fittings closed at all times. Report any damaged or inoperative fittings to the Master.

Water on deck increases the probability of downflooding through any opening. Freeing ports are fitted in bulwarks to allow water from boarding seas to drain overboard quickly. Ensure that freeing ports are unobstructed. Do not block freeing ports!

The act of lifting or hanging any weight from the vessel's crane, boom, A-frame, J-frame, etc., raises the vessel's center of gravity. As soon as the weight is lifted clear of the deck, the downward force of the weight acts at a point at the top of the weight handling equipment. If a crane is hoisting a weight over the side, the center of gravity is also shifted off center, introducing a list. When planning heavy lifts or over-the-side science operations, consult with the Master to ensure that effects of the ship's stability from such operations are within acceptable limits.

Science operations, such as towing instruments, working gear over the side or fantail, or placing heavy objects on the seafloor, can influence stability in several ways:

- The vessel may be constrained from assuming the course and speed most favorable to stability and may be subjected to icing, boarding seas, beam winds, etc.
- Working heavy weights over the side reduces stability.
- The tension of the towline or gear line may introduce a heeling moment similar to that of a beam wind.

Watertight Inter Rity

A ship's form and subdivision are calculated to provide adequate stability and resistance to damage at her design draft. These design features are defeated if the skin of the ship and subdivision bulkheads are not watertight. The original watertight integrity of a vessel is determined by its design and the quality of its construction. The proper maintenance of that integrity is a vital part of any ship's preparations to resist damage. Each undamaged tank or compartment aboard ship must be kept watertight if flooding is to be controlled and not become progressive after damage.

Know the importance of watertight fittings-strive to keep them closed when not in use. It is equally important to keep freeing ports clear. Report inoperative, damaged, or leaking fittings to the Master.

Electrical Systems/Equipment

Introduction

Individuals who work with shipboard electrical equipment must be particularly vigilant about safety, as injuries from electric shock and short circuits are too often fatal. A shipboard environment is particularly dangerous with regard to electrical systems. Because decks are made of steel and form a direct electrical path to seawater, a person touching live electrical parts would normally become a part of this circuit. The body's resistance to current flow falls with an increase in moisture level in the skin. For example, a perspiring individual working in a hot machinery space coming in contact with live electrical components would have minimal resistance to current flow and would receive much more current than a person with dry skin. This adds to the hazards of working around machinery.

Because short circuits are usually accompanied by arcs and sparking, there is always the possibility of a resulting fire. When working with electrical installations, be attentive to the risks of fire.

A 100 milliampere current can be fatal-this is about 1/1,000 of the current regularly flowing through a household light bulb. Ventricular fibrillation-the uncoordinated actions of the walls of the heart's ventricles-occurs when current flowing through the body approaches 100 milliamperes, which in turn causes the heart to stop pumping. Ventricular fibrillation will usually continue until some force is used to restore the heart's movements to a coordinated pumping action. Current flow of 200 milliamperes or higher through the body will cause severe burns and unconsciousness. It will also cause a clamping action of the heart muscles which prevents the heart from going into ventricular fibrillation. If breathing can be restored immediately, victims will often recover from these injuries.

Uugrounded Electrical System

Most shipboard electrical distribution systems *are not* grounded, and in that respect are different from household or shore systems. Neither of the two conductors in a shipboard system is grounded, while the potential between them is about 120 volts. If an individual, while grounded, were to touch either of these two conductors, that person would receive a severe shock. All live electrical circuits are always treated as potential hazards.

Personal/Scientific Equipment

Electrical equipment brought aboard for personal use, such as music systems, hair dryers, etc., should be examined by the Chief Engineer. This examination determines whether they are wired with one conductor connected to the chassis, as is common with some electronic equipment. If such equipment is used aboard a ship, it provides a hazardous path to ground for the electrical distribution system and must be rewired to the satisfaction of the Chief Engineer.

Scientific equipment (including power supplies and clean power sources) and the metal racks usually erected for stowage of scientific equipment should be properly grounded. Any discrepancies found should be reported to the Chief Engineer and remedied before such equipment is energized. Temporary electrical cables rigged for scientific equipment should be arranged to the satisfaction of the Chief Engineer. This includes marking the cable for identification and ensuring the cable is properly supported, free from possibility of chaffing, is properly protected by an overcurrent device, and is of proper size and construction for the application. Further, such cables should be removed after they have served their purpose.

Electrical Safety Practices

- **Consider the results of each act** There is absolutely no reason for individuals to take chances that will endanger their lives or the lives of others.
- **Assume circuits are live** Don't take the word of others. Stored capacitance can be fatal. Take time to test/discharge circuits before starting work.
- **Test your tester** When testing circuits to see if they are live, test a known voltage source first to see if your tester works.
- **Heed warning signs** If a sign warns that there may be two sources of power to a cabinet, take time to identify and secure both sources before reaching into the cabinet.
- **Use your senses** Be alert to smoke, overheating, and an "electrical smell" which are signs that trouble may not be far off.

- **Authorized personnel only** Only personnel authorized by the Chief Engineer should work on installed shipboard electrical equipment. Researchers should coordinate their requirements with the Chief Engineer before proceeding with work which may impact a ship's distribution system.
- **Keep covers closed** Close covers to fuse panels, junction boxes, etc., when not in use. Covers are there to keep moisture and debris out.
- **Count tools** When working in cabinets or other equipment, count the tools you take in with you and be certain that you remove the same number when you leave.
- **Beware of dual voltages** Some switchboard panels have both 450-volt and 120-volt circuits. If servicing a 120-volt circuit, beware that a higher voltage circuit is close by.
- **Remove jewelry** Don't wear jewelry when working with electrical equipment or moving machinery. Remove rings, necklaces, and bracelets when you need to work near live components. The jewelry may serve as a path to ground or cause a short circuit which could be fatal or cause injury. The same applies to metal zippers on clothing.
- **Tagged-out equipment** The ship's electricians and engineers place equipment out-of-service if it could jeopardize safety of personnel or cause equipment damage if started. Know how to secure all sources of possible power to such equipment.
- Leave equipment in working order, or tag it out-of-service before you leave.
- Do not service high-voltage equipment alone.
- Do not ground yourself. Make sure you are not grounded when adjusting equipment or using measuring equipment. Use only one hand when servicing energized equipment. Keep the other hand behind you or in your pocket.

- Don't energize wet equipment.
- Use only properly grounded power tools.
- Use fuse puller when pulling fuses.
- Examine extension cords and portable cords.

Engineering Safety and Practices

Introduction

Danger to personnel exists to some degree in every shipboard engineering operation. Because that danger is a constant companion, you may tend to discount the disastrous possibilities and ignore measures necessary to prevent accidents. Hazards to personal safety exist in virtually every system in the engineering department. High pressures and temperatures, volatile fluids, and rotating machinery which may start without notice are waiting for the unsuspecting crew member to make a mistake.

Gasoline presents a far greater hazard than diesel fuel. It must only be stored and transferred topside on weather decks. Exercise great care when fueling.

Fueling Small Boats and Engines

Fueling procedures for small boats and small engines depend on specific equipment. Fuel may be transferred from ship's tanks or drums to the boat tank by hose (diesel boats), gasoline cans may be simply placed in a boat and connected to the engine by hose (outboard-motor-driven boats), or gasoline or a gas/oil mixture may be poured from storage cans to a built-in fuel tank (portable pumps, chain saws). Whatever the method, take precautions to avoid spills, fires, or injuries. When using a transfer hose from the ship's tanks, ensure proper alignment of valves, adequate communications, and pre-established emergency procedures.

For drum or can transfers, provide drip pans under the transfer points and be cautious of overflows. When refueling portable equipment, use good judgment to prevent spills on deck or on the equipment. Never refill a tank over a hot engine. A small amount of gasoline spilled on the engine may flash and ignite the whole can with disastrous results. Contain and clean up any spills immediately.

Become familiar with the following precepts of safety:

- **Report unsafe conditions** Notify your supervisor or a ship's officer if you feel a condition, equipment, or material is unsafe.
- **Warn others** Take the time to remind shipmates of safety precautions.
- **Use protective equipment** Ear and eye protection, protective clothing, and breathing equipment are provided for your safety-use them.
- **Use safety guards** Safety guards and devices are placed on tools and equipment to prevent injury-use them correctly. If you find a safety guard missing or misaligned, inform the Chief Engineer.
- **Report injury or ill health** Report any injuries or evidence of impaired health to your supervisor or a ship's officer.
- **Exercise caution** Be alert to the hazards of the work place and take all necessary precautions.

REPAIRS

Machinery and equipment must be maintained and repaired properly. When making repairs, do it right the first time! Make-shift repairs could injure an unsuspecting person who doesn't know that the machine has been jury-rigged.

Hazardous Materials

Introduction

Research and shipboard personnel can expect to encounter hazardous materials in the form of ship's stores, paints, laboratory chemicals, cleaning agents, etc. Therefore, a working knowledge of these materials and their hazards will assist personnel in handling and storing them in a safe, responsible manner.

You are assumed to have experience and a good working knowledge of procedures for handling, storing, and disposing of hazardous materials within a shore-based laboratory. It is anticipated that you will continue your reading of the RVOC Safety Training Manual-especially Chapter 13, "Hazardous Materials," as well as resource documents that are listed therein.

Hazardous material is any substance which, because of its chemical properties, can cause the deterioration of other materials or injury to living organisms. Hazardous materials are grouped into five major classes:

- Flammable or explosive
- Corrosive
- Reactive
- Toxic or poisonous
- Cryogenic

PROTECTION

In order for hazardous materials or chemicals to harm the body, they must first gain entrance. Methods of prevention include removal or confinement of hazards, use of protective equipment, or a combination thereof.

Procedures for handling hazardous material aboard a research vessel may be different than what you are used to. Plan your experiments with minimal waste-you are limited to the storage aboard for disposal; you just don't heave HAZMAT overboard! Containers are prone to spill when the deck is moving. While at sea, some of your procedures that used to be "automatic" will have to be altered to accommodate the new environment.

Hazard Removal The best way to protect yourself from hazardous materials is to eliminate the possibility of contact. Hazard removal may be accomplished by physically removing the hazardous substance or rendering it harmless. Potential hazards can be removed or reduced by limiting the types and quantities of hazardous materials stowed and used on board and properly disposing of hazardous waste.

When presented with a spill or other hazardous situation, try to:

- Limit the spread of the hazardous material to the smallest area possible with physical barriers.
- Limit access of personnel to the hazard area and vicinity.
- Shut down or plug up the source of the hazardous material.
- Neutralize the HAZMAT with other chemicals.

Hazard Containment Hazardous materials that are carried must be properly packaged and stored to prevent injury. Storage and use areas are designed to contain or limit the spread of any spilled materials.

Personal Protective Devices Personal protective devices are worn when working with any known or unknown hazard. The skin and the respiratory tract provide only limited natural protection against harmful substances. Personal protective equipment provides a barrier between the person and the environment to prevent harmful effects from hazardous chemicals.

Laboratory Chemicals

Various forms, types, mixtures, and quantities of chemicals will be found in a laboratory. The most important factor of the use of laboratory chemicals on board a research vessel is safety. Due to the mixture of chemicals in a laboratory, there are increased hazards in these areas. There are chemicals that react with each other, water, metals, and other common items. The storage and handling of laboratory chemicals must be done carefully and by trained personnel.

When working in the lab, wear proper clothing: goggles, lab coat or coveralls, and gloves when necessary. Know the location and how to use the protective equipment on board: ventilation hoods, eye wash stations, fresh water, personal showers, and disposal units. All chemicals in the lab must be properly marked and stored in proper containers. Acids, which are highly corrosive, cannot be stored in metal containers. Any chemicals brought on board in large quantities should be stored in the appropriate lockers until they are needed. Chemicals that react with each other must not be stored in the same place; acids should not be stored with alkalis.

Any chemicals used or created on board and ready for disposal should be placed in a clearly labeled disposal unit and properly stored until port is reached. Dispose of chemicals in accordance with applicable regulatory requirements.

If a spill occurs in the lab, the personnel cleaning the spill should know what was spilled and what substances react with the spilled chemicals before cleaning. There are chemicals that will react violently with water and should be cleaned up with dry cloths. If personnel are splattered with a chemical, the affected areas should be washed with lots and water and medical attention sought.

Personal Protection

- Eye protection against irritating fumes or corrosive liquid chemicals should consist of face mask or goggles.
- Spaces that have been closed for significant periods of time should not be entered without respiratory protection until it has been established that a safe atmosphere exists.
- Full face shields, rubber gloves, rubber boots, and aprons should be worn when handling corrosive materials.
- Lab coats and goggles should be worn in the laboratories when necessary.
- Exposure to particulate matter requires the use of a respirator with an appropriate filter for protection against dust, fumes, mists, fogs, liquids, and solids.
- Protective skin cream or gloves or both should be used by handlers of sensitizers or potential skin irritants such as epoxy and polyester resins and hardeners.

Reactivity

Many chemicals that are nonhazardous in a natural state, or have a low to medium degree of hazard, can become highly hazardous when placed in contact with another chemical. The resultant mixture can be more reactive, produce more hazards, and be several times more toxic than each chemical by itself. In some cases, chemicals may react violently, even explosively, when brought together. Spontaneous explosion or heat sufficient to ignite nearby combustibles may result. Electrical currents or arcs or extreme heat can liberate or cause the formation of hazardous compounds, or the decomposition of harmless substances into hazardous materials. For example, nitrogen dioxide (NO_2) is formed by welding arcs; electrolysis in seawater releases chlorine and hydrogen gas and may produce other compounds. Oxygen in a gaseous state increases the flammable potential of other materials around it; as a liquid, it has the ability to freeze living tissue to the point of shattering. Water, when added to certain burning metals, can increase the intensity of the fire; the moisture in the air or perspiration on one's skin can cause some chemicals to ignite spontaneously.

Compressed Gases

Compressed gases such as oxygen, helium, nitrogen, and other inert gases, are used on board for many different reasons. They can be used for medical purposes, cutting and welding, weather balloons, and for laboratory experiments. Cylinders should always be kept secure. If a cylinder ruptures it could cause an explosion, feed a fire, or become a missile hazard.

Paints and Solvents

Aboard a ship, one can find a supply of paints, strippers, thinners, and cleaners (turpentine), all of which have a hazard potential. Many of the paints and solvents have low flash points, which increases the risk of fire. Paints and solvents produce toxic fumes when they are applied, drying, or removed. Wear respiratory protection and appropriate clothing (long-sleeve shirt, long pants, etc.) when painting.

Maintain proper ventilation (either natural or forced with a fan), do not smoke, and avoid using electrical equipment when applying paint and during drying and curing. Personnel handling the substance should wear respiratory mask whenever there is a risk of inhaling toxic fumes.

Radioactive Materials

Most science work using radioactive isotopes involves very low levels of radioactivity. Normally, even prolonged exposure would have no harmful effect on an individual. While spills could cause contamination or "dirty" a lab or van, these terms refer only to the negative effect on minute scientific measurements.

Radioactive materials are defined as any material or combination of materials that spontaneously emit alpha or beta rays (sometimes gamma rays) by the disintegration of the nuclei of atoms. Containers with radioactive materials must be labeled with the proper symbol for radioactive.

Keep radioactive material in one area, preferably a separate van. The working surfaces should be made of a nonporous material that is resistant to seawater and radioactive materials. Any materials that have the ability to become airborne should be worked on only in an approved fume hood.

All radioactive material should be stored in one locker clearly marked "radioactive". Radioactive materials are kept in their original containers until they are used. Solid waste materials may be stored in cans that are properly labeled and sealed. Liquid radioactive waste may be stored in plastic jars or bottles. The locker should be protected from the weather and unauthorized removal of contents. In any area where radioactive materials are being processed or handled, film badges or other exposure-measuring devices could be required and the area clearly marked "Radioactive Materials in Use." While working with isotopes, wear lab coats and gloves. Protective clothing should not leave the lab until declared radiation free. Eating, drinking, or smoking must not be permitted in areas where radioactive materials are being handled or stored. Food and beverages should never be stored near radiological laboratories or in the same refrigeration units as radioisotopes. All radioactive waste materials and any materials suspected of being contaminated should be placed in properly labeled waste containers.

In the event of a spill of radioactive material, the following general procedures should be followed:

- Keep all personnel who were in the area of the spill together until they can be tested for contamination levels. Seek qualified medical help as soon as possible.
- Block off the area where the spill occurred.
- If the clothing of personnel has been contaminated, remove and dispose of properly.
- Keep all unaffected personnel away from area until uncontaminated personnel in full protective clothing arrive to clean up the area.

MARINE SANITATION DEVICES

Marine sanitation devices (MSD) installed on board ships are used to hold or treat raw sewage and waste water. While these systems perform well in abating water pollution, the tanks and the chemical processes present hazards to personnel required to operate and maintain them.

The primary hazard to personnel from marine sanitation systems is hydrogen sulphide (H_2S) gas. This gas is invisible and has a characteristic odor of rotten eggs. It is highly toxic and flammable. Although the odor is detectable at low levels (less than 1ppm), prolong exposure to moderate levels (30-50 ppm) or brief exposure high levels (more than 100 ppm) can cause olfactory fatigue, or loss of the sense of smell. Therefore the presence of H_2S cannot always be reliably detected by its odor. At extremely high levels (500 ppm or greater), H2S acts as a systemic poison, causing unconsciousness or death due to respiratory arrest. In addition to H_2S other hazards associated with marine sanitation spills are the release of methane and other hydrocarbons, release of ammonia, reduction of oxygen in the space, and elevated levels of carbon dioxide in the air. Transfer of communicable diseases is also of great concern.

If a marine sanitation leak or spill occurs, or if the odor of H2S is detected, leave the space immediately. You may return to the area only when the space is certified to be safe.

Sources of Information

Because of the need for identification of hazardous material, two systems (NFPA 704M and DOT) for hazardous substance identification have been developed.

The NFPA 704M System is a standardized marking system which uses numbers and colors on a sign to define the three basic hazards (health, flammability, and reactivity) of a specific material. The ratings for individual chemicals can be found in the NFPA Guide to Hazardous Materials. Other references are the U.S.Coast Guard (USCG) Manual; CHRIS, Volume II; and the National Safety Council's Fundamentals of Industrial Hygiene.

DOT Hazard Identification System

The DOT Hazardous Materials Transportation Administration regulates over 1,400 hazardous materials. DOT placards and labels indicate the nature of the hazard presented by the material.

Summary

Living and working abroad a UNOLS vessel can be safe for those who know and practice safety. Emergencies must be reported and handled properly. Are you ready for this cruise? Safety is the responsibility of every person aboard- you. In the laboratory, you have learned to control the environment to ensure consistent results of your experiments. Although you cannot totally control the shipboard environment, you can control your actions and be prepared. You will be tested on this material-you will know if you've passed by the time you return home from your voyage; those who fail sometimes don't return. Have a safe and successful cruise!

Chapter 16

Understanding Shipboard

The complexity of ships, particularly of sailing ships, led to the development of a rich and various vocabulary. Many of the following terms link to more detailed discussions of nautical terminology.

- **Amidships** Toward the middle of the vessel.
- **Bow** Strictly, one of the two curved structures where the hull broadens out from the stem (the pointed end). The bows is a term for the head of the vessel or front of the ship. Compare prow, a more poetic term for the ship's head.
- **Stern** The after end of the ship.
- **Aft** Towards the stern when the relationship is within the ship.
- **Starboard** The side of the ship which lies to the right when an observer within the ship faces forward. Denoted with a green light at night.
- **Port** The side of the ship which lies to the left when an observer within the ship faces forward. (A mnemonic to distinguish port and starboard notes that left and port both have four letters. Another incorporates the navigation light: Is there any red port left?) The colour red is also a help as the port side is denoted with a red light at night.
- **(Navigation) Bridge** A structure above the weather deck, extending the full width of the vessel, which

houses a command centre, itself called by association, the bridge. A bridge usually extends a little beyond the ship's side to enable observation of boats alongside, or the proximity of a dock or lock gate; these projections are called bridge wings. In big vessels, a docking bridge used to be found aft. (See Lord, Walter. *A Night to Remember* (1976) p.96). It enabled an officer to observe docking manoeuvres before giving orders. RMS Titanic had one but they have been superseded by Closed-circuit television cameras.

- **Bulkheads** Internal "walls" in a ship. Bulkheads are the vertical equivalent of decks. They have a structural function as well as dividing spaces. They serve to prevent collapse of the hull under stress, to maintain stability (remain afloat on water by sub-division method, Naval architecture), in the event of flooding and damage, and to contain fire. Many bulkheads feature watertight doors which, in the case of certain types of ships, the crew may close remotely. An internal "wall" that is not load-bearing is usually referred to as a "partition". It is to a bulkhead as a flat is to a deck.
- **Cabin** An enclosed room on a deck or flat.
- **Capstan** A winch with a vertical axis.
- **Centre-line structure** The keel, stem, sternpost and the keelson, deadwoods, apron etc. or their modern equivalents.
- **Coaming** The raised edges of hatches and deck house's opening on decks for keeping water and articles free on the deck from falling into the hold, cabin or compartment. In the view of Naval Architect, Shipping authority or Classification society, the coaming is one of the critical criteria for the damage stability. In addition, the coaming can strengthen the structure of deck openings too.
- **Decks** The structures forming the approximately horizontal surfaces in the ship's general structure. In

a modern ship, they may be flat but used to be cambered. Unlike flats, they are a structural part of the ship.

- **Deck Head** The under-side of the deck above. Sometimes panelled over to hide the pipe work. This panelling, like that lining the bottom and sides of the holds, is the ceiling. Another common Naval term for a Deck Head is "Overhead"
- **Draft** The vertical distance from the current waterline to the lowest point of the ship or in the part of the ship under consideration.
- **Figurehead** Carved decoration at the head of a traditional sailing ship or early steamer.
- **Flat** A horizontal division inserted between decks or in the superstructure, to provide smaller accommodation such as cabins.
- A partial deck, above the upper deck and at the head of the vessel; traditionally the sailors' living quarters.
- **Freeboard** The vertical distance from the current waterline to the highest continuous watertight deck. This usually varies from one part to another.
- **Freeboard deck** The uppermost complete deck with permanent means of closing all openings in those parts which are open to the weather. In a large ship this will be the upper deck and in a smaller one, the main deck. Decks above this are superstructure.
- **Galley** The kitchen of the ship
- **Gunwale** Formerly a fabricated band placed for strengthening around the ship at the main or upper deck level to accommodate the stresses imposed by the use of artillery. In later use it is the angle between the ship's side and upper deck. It remained as a structural member, in wooden boats where it was mounted inboard of the sheer strake regardless of the need for gunnery.

- **Bulwark** The extension of the ship's side above the level of the weather deck.
- **Hold** In earlier use, below the orlop deck, the lower part of the interior of a ship's hull, especially when considered as storage space, as for cargo. In later merchant vessels it extended up through the decks to the underside of the weather deck.
- **Hull** The shell and framework of the basic flotation-oriented part of a ship
- **Keel** The central structural basis of the hull
- **Keelson** - the timber immediately above the keel of a wooden ship.
- **Mast** A spar (in a ship, a very heavy one stepped in the keelson) formerly designed for the support of one or more sails. In modern ships, it is a steel or aluminium fabrication which carries navigation lights, radar antennae etc.
- **Prow** A poetic alternative term for bows.
- **Scupper** A drainage waterway at the edge of a deck, is drained by a pipe or, on the weather deck, a small opening in the bulwarks, leading overboard. It is called a scupper which is distinct from larger openings with hinged covers on the bulwarks, designed for relieving the ship of large quantities of water in a seaway. These are called freeing ports or wash ports.
- **Stem** The upright part of the centre-line structure at the fore end of the ship.
- **Stern tube** The tube through the after end of the centre-line structure, through which the propeller shaft passes. On submarines, this may also refer to a stern-mounted torpedo tube.
- **Superstructure** The decked structure built above the freeboard deck (main or upper deck); that is, above the hull.
- **Tail shaft** A shaft (a rod or tube of metal) which transmits the power by rotary motion, from the engine to the propeller.

- A transom is a vertical (or near-vertical) flat or flattish surface that forms the stern of a vessel.
- **Weather deck** A deck which is exposed to the weather – usually either the main deck or, in larger vessels, the upper deck and forecastle and poop decks as well as parts of promenade decks, boat decks and so on in the superstructure.
- **Windlass** A winch mechanism, usually with a horizontal axis. It is used where mechanical advantage greater than that obtainable by block and tackle was needed.

Starboard

Starboard is the nautical term that refers to the right side of a vessel as perceived by a person on board the ship and facing the bow (front). Note that starboard refers to a particular and unchanging side of a ship, and thus is not a synonym for "right", a direction which is completely observer-dependent; for example, an observer on board who is facing the stern would perceive starboard to be on his left, not his right. The starboard side of a vessel is indicated with a green navigation light at night.

The origin of the term comes from old boating practices. Before ships had rudders on their centerline, they were steered by use of a specialized oar. This oar was held by a sailor located towards the stern (back) of the ship. However, like most of the rest of society, there were many more right-handed sailors than left-handed sailors. This meant that the right-handed sailors holding the steering oar (which had been broadened to provide better control) used to stand on the right side of the ship. The word starboard comes from Old English steorbord, literally meaning the side on which the ship is steered. The old English term steorbord descends from the Old Norse words stýri meaning "rudder" and borð meaning "side of a ship". The modern term "steering wheel" comes from the same language root as "starboard" or "steer board".

Similarly, the term for the left side of the boat, *port*, is derived from the practice of sailors mooring on the left side (i.e., the larboard or loading side) as to prevent the steering boards from being crushed. Because the words *larboard* and *starboard* sounded too similar to be easily distinguished, *larboard* was changed to *port*.

The starboard side of most naval vessels the world over is designated the 'senior' side. The officers' gangway or sea ladder is shipped on this side and this side of the quarterdeck is reserved for the captain. The flag or pennant of the ship's captain or senior officer in command is generally hoist on the starboard yard.

When the wind is on the starboard side of a sailing vessel, i.e. blowing *from* the right, the boat would be defined as *on starboard tack*. As a rule, sailing vessels on starboard tack are the stand on vessels, unless circumstances prevent the vessel on port tack from giving way. See International Regulations for Preventing Collisions at Sea.

Vessels at sea do not actually have any 'right of way' - they are, correctly, in the position of being 'stand on vessel' or 'give way' vessel. This means that at no time should any vessel actually navigate its way into a collision situation, and the rules are clear that no one in command of a vessel should assume a 'right of way' and should at all costs avoid a collision.

Consider two ships on courses that intersect. The rule is that the ship on the left must give way. The stand on vessel sees the green light on the starboard (right) side of the ship on the left. The give way vessel sees the red light on the port side of the stand on vessel. The helmsman gives way to a red light by either turning away and showing a stern light, or by going around the stern of the stand on vessel.

This was likely the beginning of the convention for traffic lights that use red to mean stop and green to mean go.

There are other rules governing which is a stand on vessel, such as small ships giving way to big ships, powered ships giving way to sailing ships, and in some circumstances vessels under sail giving way to powered vessels that are constrained by their draught, or restricted in their ability to manoeuvre.

Therefore the green light does not mean an unqualified go, but rather it means proceed with caution subject to other rules applying. The earliest railway signals went red/green/white for stop/caution/go following this naval practice and were only later changed to the more familiar red/yellow/green.

The very simple application of red light and green light is that if the helmsman sees a red light, the helmsman should make sure that the other vessel can see his red light, which usually means giving way. If he sees a green light, he should stand on, but without getting into a collision situation.

The sailing rules that dictate that a sailing vessel on starboard tack (the side the wind is coming from) is the stand on vessel is as old as any other regulations. Likewise, if on the same tack, a sailing vessel that is upwind of another is the give way vessel. On square rigs, the business of tacking was called 'wearing ship' (something like a gybe), involved a huge loss of searoom, and could take ten minutes or more to complete.

Bridge of a ship

The bridge of a ship is an area or room where the ship's navigational controls and other essential equipment related to ship operations are housed and operated. It is so called because it once was a bridge between paddlewheel housings on either side of early steamboats. This new vantage point was deemed so convenient that it was retained after the paddlewheels were superseded.

The bridge is especially useful when the ship is to be brought against a dock as it will usually extend out far enough so that the entire side of the ship may be viewed. The pilot house was initially only a small shelter on an otherwise open bridge, but since modern ships typically extend the pilot house across most or all of the span of the bridge, the two terms are now usually interchangeable.

When a ship is underway, the ship's captain or a senior officer is on the bridge at all times to maintain command and control.

Cabin

A cabin is an enclosed room generally on a ship or an aircraft.

In sailing ships, the officers and paying passengers would have an individual or shared cabin.

The commanding officer also known as the captain would have the grand cabin that normally spanned the stern with large windows, subdivided with movable panels that could be taken down in time of battle so that a small gun could be set up there or the large room used as an operating theatre.

Deck (ship)

A deck is a permanent covering over a compartment or a hull[1] of a ship. On a boat or ship, the primary deck is the horizontal structure which forms the 'lid' of the hull, which both strengthens the hull and serves as the primary working surface. Vessels often have more than one level both within the hull and in the superstructure above the primary deck which are similar to the floors of a multi-story building, and which are also referred to as decks, as are specific compartments and decks built over specific areas of the superstructure.

The purpose of the primary deck is structural, and only secondarily to provide weather-tightness, and to support people and equipment. The deck serves as the lid to the complex box girder which is the hull. It resists tension, compression, and racking forces. The deck's scantling is usually the same as the topsides, or might be heavier if the deck is expected to carry heavier loads (for example a container ship). The deck will be reinforced around deck fittings such as the capstan, cleats, or bollards.

On ships with more than one level, deck refers to the level itself. The actual floor surface is called the sole, while the term floor refers to a structural member tying the ships frames or ribs together over the keel. In modern ships, the interior decks are usually numbered from the primary deck, which is #1, downward and upward. So the first deck below the primary deck will be #2, and the first above the primary deck will be #A2 or #S2 (for "Above" or "Superstructure"). However, ships may also call decks by common names, or (especially on cruise ships) may invent fanciful and romantic names for a specific deck or area of that specific ship, such as the Lido deck of the Princess Lines' Love Boat.

Equipment mounted on deck, such as the ship's wheel, binnacle, fife rails, and so forth, may be collectively referred to as deck furniture. Weather decks in western designs evolved from having structures fore and aft (forecastles and cabins) to mostly clear, then in the 19th century pilothouses and deckhouses began to appear, eventually developing into the superstructure of modern ships. Eastern designs developed earlier, with efficient middle decks and minimalist fore and aft cabin structures across a range of designs.

Common Names for Decks

In vessels having more than one deck there are various naming conventions, numerically, alphabetically, etc. However, there are also a variety of common historical names and types of decks:

- **Berth deck**: [*Naval*] A deck next below the gun deck, where the hammocks of the crew are swung.
- **Boat deck**: Especially on ships with sponsons, the deck area where lifeboats or the ship's gig are stored.
- **Boiler deck**: (River Steamers) The deck on which the boilers are placed.
- **Bridge deck**: (a) The deck area including the helm and navigation station, and where the Officer on deck will be found, also known as the **Con** (b) An athwartships structure at the forward end of the cockpit with a deck, often somewhat lower than the primary deck, to prevent a pooping wave from entering through the companionway.
- **Flush deck**: Any continuous, unbroken deck from stem to stern.

- **Gun deck**: [*Naval*] a deck below the spar deck, on which the ship's guns are carried. If there are two gun decks, the upper one is called the main deck, the lower, the lower gun deck; if there are three, one is called the middle gun deck.
- **Half-deck**: That portion of the deck next below the spar deck which is between the mainmast and the cabin.
- **Helo deck**: Usually located near the stern and always kept clear of obstacles hazardous to a helicopter landing.
- **Hurricane deck**: (River Steamers, etc.), the upper deck, usually a light deck, erected above the frame of the hull.
- **Middle or Waist deck** The upper deck amidships, the working area of the deck.
- **Orlop deck**: The deck or part of a deck where the cables are stowed, usually below the water line. It is the lowest deck in a ship.
- **Poop deck**: The deck forming the roof of a poop or poop cabin, built on the upper deck and extending from the mizzenmast aft.
- **Promenade deck**: A "wrap-around porch" found on passenger ships and riverboats encircling the superstructure.
- **Quarter-deck**: (a) The part of the upper deck abaft the mainmast, including the poop deck when there is one. Usually reserved for ship's officers, guests, and passengers. (b) [*Naval*] The area to which a gangway for officers and diplomatic guests to board the vessel leads. Also any entry point for personnel.
- **Side-decks**: The upper decks outboard of any structures such as a coachroof or doghouse, also called a breezeway
- **Spar deck**: (a) Same as the upper deck. (b) Sometimes a light deck fitted over the upper deck.

- **Sweep deck**: [*Naval*] The aftmost deck on a minesweeper, set close to the waterline for ease in lauch and recovery of equipment.
- **Upper deck**: The highest deck of the hull, extending from stem to stern.
- **Weather deck**: (a) Any deck exposed to the outside. (b) The windward side decks.

Construction

Methods in Wood

A traditional wood deck would consist of planks laid fore and aft over beams and along carlins, the seams of which are caulked and payed with tar. A yacht or other fancy boat might then have the deck canvased, with the fabric laid down in a thick layer of paint or sealant, and additional coats painted over. The wash or apron boards form the joint between the deck planking and that of the topsides, and are caulked similarly.

Modern "constructed decks" are used primarily on fibreglass, composite, and cold-molded hulls. The under structure of beams and carlins is the same as above. The decking itself is usually multiple layers of marine-grade plywood, covered over with layers of fibreglass in a plastic resin such as epoxy or polyester overlapped onto the topsides of the hull.

Methods in Metal

Generally speaking, the method outlined for "constructed decks" is most similar to metal decks. The deck plating is laid over metal beams and carlins and tacked temporarily in place. The difficulty in metal construction is avoiding distortion of the plate while welding due to the high heat involved in the process. Welds are usually double pass, meaning each seam is welded twice, a time consuming process which may take longer than building the wood deck. But welds result in a waterproof deck which is strong and easily repairable. The deck structure is welded to the hull, making it structurally a single unit.

Because a metal deck, painted to reduce corrosion, can be quite slippery as well as picking up heat from the sun and being quite loud to work on, often a layer of wood decking or thick non-skid paint are applied to its surface.

Methods in Fiberglass

The process for building a deck in fibreglass is the same as for building a hull: a female mould is built, a layer of gel coat is sprayed in, then layers of fibreglass in resin are built up to the required deck thickness (if the deck has a core, the outer skin layers of fibreglass and resin are laid, then the core material, and finally the inner skin layers.) The deck is removed from the mould and usually mechanically fastened to the hull.

Fibreglass decks are quite slick with their mirror-smooth surfaces, so a non-skid texture is often moulded into their surface, or non-skid pads glued down in working areas.

Rules of Thumb to Determine the Deck Scantlings

The thickness of the decking affects how strong the hull is, and is directly related to how thick the skin of the hull itself is, which is of course related to how large the vessel is, the kind of work it is expected to do, and the kind of weather it may reasonably be expected to endure. While a Naval Engineer or Architect may have precise methods of determining what the scantlings should be, traditional builders used previous experiences and simpler rules-of-thumb to determine how thick the deck should be built.

The numbers derived by these forumlae gives a rough number for determining the average thickness of materials based on some crude hull measurements. Below the waterline the thickness should be approximately 115% of the result, while upper topsides and decks might be reduced to 85% of the result.

- In wood - For plank thickness in inches, LOA (Length OverAll) and Beam are measured in feet. For plank thickness in mm, LOA and Beam are measured in meters.

- Plank thickness in inches = $\frac{\sqrt{LOA} + Beam}{16}$
- Plank thickness in mm =
  $\left[\sqrt{LOA * 3.28} + (Beam * 3.28) * 1.58\right]$

- In fiberglass - For skin thickness in inches, LWL (Length WaterLine) is in feet. For skin thickness in mm, LWL is in meters.
  - Skin thickness (inches) = $0.07 + \frac{LWL}{150}$
  - Skin thickness (mm) = $1.8 + \frac{LWL}{18}$
- In fiberglass sandwiche - First determine the skin thickness as single skin, then multiply by modifiers for inner skin, outer skin, and core thicknesses. Cored decks might be modified even thicker, 2.6-2.7, to increase stiffness.
  - Inner skin modifier = 0.3
  - Outer skin modifier = 0.4
  - Core modifier = 2.2

Modern Warships

In most modern warships the commanding officer has a main cabin, often adjacent to the ship's central control room (operations room), and a sea cabin adjacent to the bridge. Thus, when likely to be called from sleep or attending to administration, the CO can be at the Bridge or Ops room instantly.

In the Star Trek science fiction series, the sea cabin has become the ready room which amply describes its relationship to the bridge and the captain's use of it.

Officers will normally have their own cabins, which doubles as their office. Some senior non-commissioned officers may have a cabin for similar reasons.

In ships carrying passengers, they are normally accommodated in cabins, taking the terminology familiar to seafarers and so adding mystique to a voyage.

Chapter 17

International Maritime Organization and Safety

International Maritime Organization (IMO): Formerly known as the Inter-Governmental Maritime Consultative Organization (IMCO), was established in 1948 through the United Nations to coordinate international maritime safety and related practices. However the IMO did not enter into full force until 1958.

Headquartered in London, U.K., the IMO promotes cooperation among governments and the shipping industry to improve maritime safety and to prevent marine pollution. IMO is governed by an Assembly of members and is financially administered by a Council of members elected from the Assembly. The work of IMO is conducted through five committees and these are supported by technical sub-committees. Member organizations of the UN organizational family may observe the proceedings of the IMO. Observer status may be granted to qualified non-governmental organizations.

The IMO is supported by a permanent secretariat of employees who are representative of its members. The secrectariat is composed of a Secretary-General who is periodically elected by the Assembly, and various divisions including, inter alia, marine safety, environmental protection, and a conference section.

The concept of IMO was born after the RMS *Titanic* disaster. By modern standards, the design of the *Titanic* made her appallingly vulnerable. Her "watertight" bulkheads, by design, did not extend all the way to the overhead because the engineers calculated that it was impossible for the ship to take on a trim or list sufficient for water to cascade over their tops if the bulkheads were of a certain height.

When *Titanic* struck the iceberg, these calculations were proven dismally incorrect. When people began abandoning ship, it became obvious that not nearly enough lifeboats were available. Many lives and much money were lost in this tragedy.

Up until that time, each nation had made its own rules about ship design, construction, and safety equipment. The *Inter-Governmental Maritime Consultative Organization (IMCO)* was formed in response to the *Titanic* event, but was "put on the back burner" when World War I broke out. After the war ended, IMCO was revived and produced a group of regulations concerning shipbuilding and safety called "Safety Of Life At Sea"..."SOLAS". Through the years, SOLAS has been modified and upgraded to adapt to changes in technology and lessons learned.

IMCO eventually became IMO. IMO regularly enacts regulations (such as the International Regulations for Preventing Collisions at Sea) which are enforced by class societies and recognized organizations who survey ships regularly to ensure compliance with specific laws applicable to each individual ship. Port State Control authority was enacted, allowing such agencies as the US and British coast guards to inspect foreign flag ships calling at ports of the many port states. Memoranda of Understanding (protocols)were signed by some countries unifying Port State Control procedures among the signators.

Of course, the numbers will never be known, but IMO has protected countless lives, saved enormous amounts of money, and prevented numerous environmental disasters over the years.

Legal Instruments

IMO is the source of approximately 60 legal instruments that guide the regulatory development of its member states to improve safety at sea, facilitate trade among seafaring states and protect the maritime environment. The most well known being the Safety of Life at Sea Convention (SOLAS).

Current Issues

Recent initiatives at the IMO have included amendments to the Safety of Life at Sea Convention (SOLAS), which upgraded fire protection standards on passenger ships, the International Convention on Standards of Training, Certification and Watchkeeping for Seafarers (STCW) which establishes basic requirements on training, certification and watchkeeping for seafarers and to the Convention on the Prevention of Maritime Pollution (MARPOL 73/78), which required double hulls on all tankers. All these initiatives were instigated by representatives of the United States before the IMO.

Prior to 11 September 2001, IMO had begun work on the International Ship and Port Security Code, which was designed to provide guidance for shipowners and port facilities in establishing strict security procedures to prevent weapons of mass destruction and other contraband from being transported by ship. The events of 9/11 created greater urgency to this effort and, in December 2002, new amendments to the 1974 SOLAS Convention were enacted. These amendments gave rise to the International Ship and Port Security Code, which went into effect on 1 July 2004.

The ISPS Code required most ships and port facilities engaged in international trade to establish and maintain strict security procedures as specified in ship and port specific Ship Security Plans and Port Facility Security Plans. The concept of the Code is to provide layered and redundant defenses against smuggling, terrorism, piracy, stowaways, etc.

The IMO is also responsible for publishing the International Code of Signals for use between merchant and naval vessels.

Global Maritime Distress Safety System

The Global Maritime Distress Safety System (GMDSS) is an internationally agreed-upon set of safety procedures, types of equipment, and communication protocols used to increase safety and make it easier to rescue distressed ships, boats and aircraft.

GMDSS consists of several systems, some of which are new, but many of which have been in operation for many years. The system is intended to perform the following functions: alerting (including position determination of the unit in distress), search and rescue coordination, locating (homing), maritime safety information broadcasts, general communications, and bridge-to-bridge communications. Specific radio carriage requirements depend upon the ship's area of operation, rather than its tonnage. The system also provides redundant means of distress alerting, and emergency sources of power.

Index

D

E

F

G

H

I

K

L

M

N

O

P

V

W

Y

Z